'Mark Rutherford' was the pseudonym of William Hale White. Hale White was born in Bedford in 1831 and his childhood there inspired many of his books, while his father William instilled White's love of literature, his radical socialism and his profound if defiant religious faith.

White trained as a nonconformist minister until 1852, but was expelled from New College, London for unorthodox views. He then worked, alongside George Eliot, for the *Westminster Review*, though in 1854 he rejected an offer of partnership and entered the Registrar-General's as a clerk; he stayed in the Civil Service almost forty years.

From 1861 until 1883 White supplemented his income by contributing columns to provincial newspapers and writing occasional pieces. He was fifty-two before he published his first major book, a translation of Spinoza's *Ethic*. This was followed by five others while he was still working, and another fourteen after he retired in 1892. The letters, criticism, translations appeared under his own name, but the journals and novels – *The Autobiography of Mark Rutherford* (1881), *Mark Rutherford's Deliverance* (1885), *The Revolution in Tanner's Lane* (1887), *Miriam's Schooling* (1890), *Catharine Furze* and *Clara Hopgood* (1896), all being published by The Hogarth Press – were penned by 'Mark Rutherford'. To confuse matters further, White invented a fictitious editor for 'Mark Rutherford' – 'Reuben Shapcott'. Behind these two alter egos the real author hid for many years until, in 1896, the columnist Claudius Clear (W. Robertson Nicholl) revealed Hale White as the only begetter of these works.

Twenty years after the death of his first wife, Harriet, Hale White married the writer Dorothy Vernon White in 1911. He died at Groombridge in 1913.

CATHARINE FURZE

Mark Rutherford

New Afterword by
Claire Tomalin

THE HOGARTH PRESS
LONDON

Published in 1985 by
The Hogarth Press
40 William IV Street, London WC2N 4DF

First published in Great Britain by T. Fisher Unwin 1893
Reset for the Hogarth edition
Afterword copyright © Claire Tomalin 1985

British Library Cataloguing in Publication Data
Rutherford, Mark
Catharine Furze
Rn: William Hale White   I. Title
823'.8[F]   P'r5795.W7
ISBN 0 7012 1918 1

Printed in Great Britain by
Cox & Wyman Ltd
Reading, Berkshire

CHAPTER I

It was a bright, hot, August Saturday in the market town of Eastthorpe, in the eastern Midlands, in the year 1840. Eastthorpe lay about five miles on the western side of the Fens, in a very level country on the banks of a river, broad and deep, but with only just sufficient fall to enable its long-lingering waters to reach the sea. It was an ancient market town, with a six-arched stone bridge, and with a High Street from which three or four smaller and narrower streets connected by courts and alleys diverged at right angles. In the middle of the town was the church, an immense building, big enough to hold half Eastthorpe, and celebrated for its beautiful spire and its peal of eight bells. Round the church lay the churchyard, fringed with huge elms, and in the Abbey Close, as it was called, which was the outer girdle of the churchyard on three sides, the fourth side of the square being the High Street, there lived in 1840 the principal doctor, the lawyer, the parson, and two aged gentlewomen with some property, who were daughters of one of the former partners in the bank, had been born in Eastthorpe, and had scarcely ever quitted it. Here also were a young ladies' seminary and an ancient grammar school for the education of forty boys, sons of freemen of the town. The houses in the Close were not of the same class as the rest; they were mostly old red brick, with white sashes, and they all had gardens, long, narrow, and shady, which, on the south side of the Close, ran down to the river. One of these houses was even older, black-timbered, gabled, plastered, the sole remains, saving the church, of Eastthorpe as it was in the reign of Henry the Eighth.

Just beyond the church, going from the bridge, the High Street was so wide that the houses on either side were separated by a space of over two hundred feet. This elongated space was the market-place. In the centre was the Moot Hall, a quaint little

building, supported on oak pillars, and in the shelter underneath the farmers assembled on market day. All round the Moot
Hall, and extending far up and down the street, were cattle-pens
and sheep-pens, which were never removed. Most of the shops
were still bow-windowed, with small panes of glass, but the first
innovation, indicative of the new era at hand, had just been
made. The druggist, as a man of science and advanced ideas,
had replaced his bow-window with plate-glass, had put a cornice
over it, had stuccoed his bricks, and had erected a kind of
balustrade of stucco, so as to hide as much as possible the attic
windows, which looked over, meekly protesting. Nearly
opposite the Moot Hall was the Bell Inn, the principal inn in the
town. There were other inns, respectable enough, such as the
Bull, a little higher up, patronised by the smaller commercial
travellers and farmers, but the entrance passage to the Bull had
sand on the floor, and carriers made it a house of call. To the Bell
the two coaches came which went through Eastthorpe, and
there they changed horses. Both the Bull and the Bell had
market dinners, but at the Bell the charge was three-and-
sixpence; sherry was often drunk, and there the steward to the
Honourable Mr Eaton, the principal landowner always met the
tenants. The Bell was Tory and the Bull was Whig, but no
stranger of respectability, Whig or Tory, visiting Eastthorpe
could possibly hesitate about going to the Bell, with its large
gilded device projecting over the pathway, with its broad
archway at the side always freshly gravelled, and its handsome
balcony on the first floor, from which the Tory county can-
didates, during election times, addressed the free and
independent electors and cattle.

Eastthorpe was a malting town, and down by the water were
two or three large malthouses. The view from the bridge was not
particularly picturesque, but it was pleasant, especially in
summer, when the wind was south-west. The malthouses and
their cowls, the wharves and the gaily painted sailing barges
alongside, the fringe of slanting willows turning the silver-grey
sides of their foliage towards the breeze, the island in the middle
of the river with bigger willows, the large expanse of sky, the soft
clouds distinct in form almost to the far distant horizon, and,

looking eastwards, the illimitable distance towards the fens and the sea – all this made up a landscape, more suitable perhaps to some persons than rock or waterfall, although no picture had ever been painted of it, and nobody had ever come to see it.

Such was Eastthorpe. For hundreds of years had the shadow of St Mary's swept slowly over the roofs underneath it, and, of all those years, scarcely a line of its history survived, save what was written in the churchyard or in the church registers. The town had stood for the Parliament in the days of the Civil War, and there had been a skirmish in the place; but who fought in it, who were killed in it, and what the result was, nobody knew. Half a dozen old skulls of much earlier date and of great size were once found in a gravel pit two miles away, and were the subject of much talk, some taking them for Romans, some for Britons, some for Saxons, and some for Danes. As it was impossible to be sure if they were Christian, they could not be put in consecrated ground; they were therefore included in an auction of dead and live stock, and were bought by the doctor. Surnames survived in Eastthorpe with singular pertinacity, for it was remote from the world, but what was the relationship between the scores of Thaxtons, for example, whose deaths were inscribed on the tombstones, some of them all awry and weather-worn, and the Thaxtons of 1840, no living Thaxton could tell, every spiritual trace of them having disappeared more utterly than their bones. Their bones, indeed, did not disappear, and were a source of much trouble to the sexton, for in digging a new grave they came up to the surface in quantities, and had to be shovelled in and covered up again, so that the bodily remains of successive generations were jumbled together, and Puritan and Georgian Thaxtons were mixed promiscuously with their descendants. Nevertheless, East-thorpe had really had a history. It had known victory and defeat, love, hatred, intrigue, hope, despair, and all the passions, just as Elizabeth, King Charles, Cromwell, and Queen Anne knew them, but they were not recorded.

It was a bright, hot, August Saturday, as we have said, and it was market day. Furthermore, it was half-past two in the afternoon, and the guests at Mr Furze's had just finished their

3

dinner. Mr Furze was the largest ironmonger in Eastthorpe, and sold not only ironmongery, but ploughs and all kinds of agricultural implements. At the back of the shop was a small foundry where all the foundry work for miles round Eastthorpe was done. It was Mr Furze's practice always to keep a kind of open house on Saturday, and on this particular day, at half-past two, Mr Bellamy, Mr Chandler, Mr Gosford, and Mr Furze were drinking their whiskey-and-water and smoking their pipes in Mr Furze's parlour. The first three were well-to-do farmers, and with them the whiskey-and-water was not a pretence. Mr Furze was a tradesman, and of a different build. Strong tobacco and whiskey at that hour and in that heat were rather too much for him, and he played with his pipe and drank very slowly. The conversation had subsided for a while under the influence of the beef, Yorkshire pudding, beer, and spirits, when Mr Bellamy observed –

'Old Bartlett's widow still a-livin' up at the Croft?'

'Yes,' said Mr Gosford, after filling his pipe again and pausing for at least a minute, 'Bartlett's dead.'

'Bartlett wur a slow-coach,' observed Mr Chandler, after another pause of a minute, 'so wur his mare. I mind me I wur behind his mare about five year ago last Michaelmas, and I wur well-nigh perished. I wur a-goin' to give her a poke with my stick, and old Bartlett says, "Doan't hit her, doan't hit her; yer can't alter her." '

The three worthy farmers roared with laughter; Mr Furze smiling gently.

'That was a good 'un,' said Mr Bellamy.

'Ah,' replied Chandler, 'I mind that as well as if it wur yesterday.'

Mr Bellamy at this point had to leave, and Mr Furze was obliged to attend to his shop. Gosford and Chandler, however, remained, and Gosford continued the subject of Bartlett's widow.

'What's she a-stayin' on for up there?'

'Old Bartlett's left her a goodish bit.'

'She wur younger than he.'

A dead silence of some minutes.

4

'She ain't a-goin' to take the Croft on herself,' observed Gosford.

'Them beasts of the squire's,' replied Chandler, 'fetched a goodish lot. Scaled just over ninety stone apiece.'

'Why doan't you go in for the widow, Chandler?'

Mr Chandler was a widower.

'Eh!' (with a nasal tone and a smile) – 'bit too much for me.'

'Too much? Why, there ain't above fourteen stone of her. Keep yer warm o' nights up at your cold place.'

Mr Chandler took the pipe out of his mouth, put it inside the fender, compressed his lips, rubbed his chin, and looked up to the ceiling.

'Well, I must be a-goin'.'

'I suppose I must too,' and they both went their ways, to meet again at tea-time.

At five punctually all had again assembled, the additions to the party being Mrs Furze and her daughter Catharine, a young woman of nineteen. Mrs Furze was not an Eastthorpe lady; she came from Cambridge, and Mr Furze had first seen her when she was on a visit in Eastthorpe. Her father was a draper in Cambridge, which was not only a much bigger place than Eastthorpe, but had a university, and Mrs Furze talked about the university familiarly, so that, although her education had been slender, a university flavour clung to her, and the farmers round Eastthorpe would have been quite unable to determine the difference between her and a senior wrangler, if they had known what a senior wrangler was.

'Ha,' observed Mr Gosford, when they were seated, 'I wur sayin', Mrs Furze, to Chandler as he ought to go in for old Bartlett's widow. Now what do *you* think? Wouldn't they make a pretty pair?' and he twisted Chandler's shoulders round a little till he faced Mrs Furze.

'Don't you be a fool, Gosford,' said Chandler in good temper, but, as he disengaged himself, he upset his tea on Mrs Furze's carpet.

'Really, Mr Gosford,' replied Mrs Furze, with some dignity and asperity, 'I am no judge in such matters. They are best left to the persons concerned.'

'No offence, ma'am, no offence.'

Mrs Furze was not quite a favourite with her husband's friends, and he knew it, but he was extremely anxious that their dislike to her should not damage his business relationships with them. So he endeavoured to act as mediator.

'No doubt, my dear, no doubt, but at the same time there is no reason why Mr Gosford should not make any suggestion which may be to our friend Chandler's advantage.'

But Mr Gosford was checked, and did not pursue the subject. Catharine sat next to him.

'Mr Gosford, when may I come to Moat Farm again?'

'Lord, my dear, whenever you like; you know that. Me and Mrs G. is always glad to see you. *When*ever you please,' and Mr Gosford instantly recovered the good-humour which Mrs Furze had suppressed.

'Don't forget us,' chimed in Mr Bellamy. 'We'll turn out your room and store apples in it if you don't use it oftener.'

'Now, Mr Bellamy,' said Catharine, holding up her finger at him, 'you'll be sick of me at last. You've forgotten when I had that bad cold at your house, and was in bed there for a week, and what a bother I was to Mrs Bellamy.'

'Bother!' cried Bellamy – 'bother! Lord have mercy on us! why the missus was sayin' when you talked about bother, my missus says, "I'd sooner have Catharine here, and me have tea up there with her, notwithstanding there must be a fire upstairs and I've had to send Lucy to the infirmary with a whitlow on her thumb – yes, I would, than be at a many tea-parties I know." '

Mrs Furze gave elaborate tea-parties, and was uncomfortably uncertain whether or not the shaft was intended for her.

'My dear Catharine, I shall be delighted if you go either to Mr Gosford's or to Mr Bellamy's, but you must consider your wardrobe a little. You will remember that the last time on each occasion a dress was torn in pieces.'

'But, mother, are not dresses intended to keep thorns from our legs; or, at any rate, isn't that *one* reason why we wear them?'

'Suppose it to be so, my dear, there is no reason why you should plunge about in thorns.'

'No.'

Catharine had a provoking way of saying 'yes' or 'no' when she wished to terminate a controversy. She stated her own opinion, and then, if objection was raised, at least by some people, her father and mother included, she professed agreement by a simple monosyllable, either because she was lazy, or because she saw that there was no chance of further profit in the discussion. It was irritating, because it was always clear she meant nothing. At this instant a servant opened the door, and Alice, a curly brown retriever, squeezed herself in, and made straight for Catharine, putting her head on Catharine's lap.

'Catharine, Catharine!' cried her mother, with a little scream, 'she's dripping wet. Do pray, my child, think of the carpet.'

But Catharine put her lips to Alice's face and kissed it deliberately, giving her a piece of cake.

'Mr Gosford, my poor bitch has puppies – three of them – all as true as their mother, for we know the father.'

'Ah!' replied Gosford, 'you're lucky, then, Miss Catharine, for dogs, especially in a town –'

Mrs Furze at this moment hastily rang the bell, making an unusual clatter with the crockery: Mr Furze said the company must excuse him, and the three worthy farmers rose to take their departure.

CHAPTER II

It was Mr Furze's custom on Sunday to go to sleep for an hour between dinner and tea upstairs in what was called the drawing-room, while Mrs Furze sat and read, or said she read, a religious book. On hot summer afternoons Mr Furze always took off his coat before he had his nap, and sometimes divested himself of his waist-coat. When the coat and waistcoat were taken off, Mrs Furze invariably drew down the blinds. She had often remonstrated with her husband for appearing in his shirt-sleeves, and objected to the neighbours seeing him in this costume. There was a sofa in the room, but it was horsehair, with high ends both alike, not comfortable, which were covered with curious complications called antimacassars, that slipped off directly they were touched, so that anybody who leaned upon them was engaged continually in warfare with them, picking them up from the floor or spreading them out again. There was also an easy chair, but it was not easy, for it matched the sofa in horse-hair, and was so ingeniously contrived, that directly a person placed himself in it, it gently shot him forwards. Furthermore, it had special antimacassars, which were a work of art, and Mrs Furze had warned Mr Furze off them. 'He would ruin them,' she said, 'if he put his head upon them.' So a windsor chair with a high back was always carried by Mr Furze upstairs after dinner, together with a common kitchen chair, and on these he slumbered. The room was never used, save on Sundays and when Mrs Furze gave a tea-party. It overlooked the market-place, and, although on a Sunday after-noon the High Street was almost completely silent, Mrs Furze liked to sit so near the window that she could peep out at the edge of the blind when she was not dozing. It is true no master nor mistress ever stirred at that hour, but every now and then a maidservant could be seen, and she was better than nothing for the purpose of criticism. A round table stood in the middle of the room with a pink vase on it containing artificial flowers, and on the mantelpiece were two other pink vases and two great shells. Over the mantelpiece was a portrait of His Majesty King George the Fourth in his robes, and exactly opposite was a picture of the Virgin Mary, which was old and valuable. Mr Furze bought it at a sale with some other things, and did not quite like it. It savoured of Popery, which he could not abide; but the parson one day saw it and told Mrs Furze it was worth something; whereupon she put it in a new maple frame, and had it hung in a place of honour second to that occupied by King George, and so arranged that he and the Virgin were always looking at one another. On the other side of the room were a likeness of Mr Eaton in hunting array, with the dogs, and a mezzotint of the Deluge.

Mr Furze had just awaked on the Sunday afternoon following the day of which the history is partly given in the first chapter.

'My dear,' said his wife, 'I have been thinking a good deal of Catharine. She is not quite what I could wish.'

'No,' replied Mr Furze, with a yawn.

'To begin with, she uses bad language. I was really quite shocked yesterday to hear the extremely vulgar word, almost – almost – I do not know what to call it – profane, I may say, which she applied to her dog when talking of it to Mr Gosford. Then she goes in the foundry; and I firmly believe that all the money which has been spent on her music is utterly thrown away.'

'The thing is – what is to be done?'

'Now, I have a plan.'

In order to make Mrs Furze's plan fully intelligible, it may be as well to explain that, up to the year 1840, the tradesmen of Eastthorpe had lived at their shops. But a year or two before that date some houses had been built at the north end of the town and called 'The Terrace.' A new doctor had taken one, the brewer another, and a third had been taken by the grocer, a man reputed to be very well off, who not only did a large retail business, but supplied the small shops in the villages round.

'Well, my dear, what is your plan?'

'Your connection is extending, and you want more room.

9

Now, why should you not move to the Terrace? If we were to go there, Catharine would be withdrawn from the society in which she at present mixes. You could not continue to give market dinners, and gradually her acquaintance with the persons whom you now invite would cease. I believe, too, that if we were in the Terrace Mrs Colston would call on us. As the wife of a brewer, she cannot do so now. Then there is just another thing which has been on my mind for a long time. It is settled that Mr Jennings is to leave, for he has accepted an invitation from the cause at Ely. I do not think we shall like anybody after Mr Jennings, and it would be a good opportunity for us to exchange the chapel for the church. We have attended the chapel regularly, but I have always felt a kind of prejudice there against us, or at least against myself, and there is no denying that the people who go to church are vastly more genteel, and so are the service and everything about it – the vespers – the bells – somehow there is a respectability in it.'

Mr Furze was silent. At last he said, 'It is a very serious matter. I must consider it in all its bearings.'

It *was* a serious matter, and he did consider it – but not in all its bearings, for he did nothing but think about it, so that it enveloped him, and he could not put himself at such a distance that he could see its real shape. He was now well over fifty, and was the kind of person with whom habits become firmly fixed. He was fixed even in his dress. He always wore a white neckcloth, and his shirt was frilled – fashions which were already beginning to die out in Eastthorpe. His manner of life was most regular: breakfast at eight, dinner at one, tea at five, supper at nine with a pipe afterwards, was his unvarying round. He never left Eastthorpe for a holiday, and read no books of any kind. He was a most respectable member of a Dissenting congregation, but he was not a member of the church, and was never seen at the week-night services or the prayer-meetings. He went through the ceremony of family worship morning and evening, but he did not pray extempore, as did the elect, and contented himself with reading prayers from a book called 'Family Devotions'. The days were over for Eastthorpe when a man like Mr Furze could be denounced, a man who paid his pew-rent regularly, and contributed to the missionary societies. The days were over when any expostulations could be addressed to him, or any attempts made to bring him within the fold, and Mr Jennings therefore called on him, and religion was not mentioned. It may seem extraordinary that, without convictions based on any reasoning process, Mr Furze's outward existence should have been so correct and so moral. He had passed through the usually stormy period of youth without censure. It is true he was married young, but before his marriage nobody had ever heard a syllable against him, and, after marriage, he never drank a drop too much, and never was guilty of a single dishonest action. Day after day passed by like all preceding days, in unbroken, level succession, without even the excitement of meeting-house emotion. Naturally, therefore, his wife's proposals made him uneasy, and even alarmed him. He shrank from them unconsciously, and yet his aversion was perfectly wise; more so, perhaps, than any action for which he could have assigned a definite motive. With men like Mr Furze the unconscious reason, which is partly a direction by past and forgotten experiences, and partly instinct, is often more to be trusted than any mental operation, strictly so-called. An attempt to use the mind actively on subjects which are too large, or with which it has not been accustomed to deal, is pretty nearly sure to mislead. He knew, or it knew, whatever we like to call it, that to break him from his surroundings meant that he himself was to be broken, for they were a part of him.

His wife attacked him again the next day. She was bent upon moving, and it is only fair to her to say that she did really wish to go for Catharine's sake. She loved the child in her own way, but she also wanted to go for many other reasons.

'Well, my dear, what have you to say to my little scheme?'

'How about my dinner and tea?'

'Come home to the Terrace. How far is it? Ten minutes' walk.'

'An hour every day, in all weathers; and then there's the expense.'

'As to the expense, I am certain we should save in the long run, because you would not be expected to be continually asking people to meals.'

'I am afraid that the business might suffer.'

'Nonsense! In what way, my dear? Your attention will be more fixed upon it than it can be with the parlour always behind you.'

There was something in that, and Mr Furze was perplexed. He was not sufficiently well educated to know that something, and a great deal, too, can be said for anything, and he had not arrived at that callousness to argument which is the last result of culture.

'Yes, but I was thinking that perhaps if we leave off chapel and go to church some of our customers may not like it.'

'Now, my good man, Furze, why you know you have as many customers who go to church as to chapel.'

'Ah! but those who go to chapel may drop off.'

'Why should they? We have plenty of customers who go to church. They don't leave us because we are Dissenters, and, as there are five times as many church people as Dissenters, your connection will be extended.'

Mrs Furze was unanswerable, but her poor husband, after all, was right. The change, when it took place, did not bring more people to the shop, and some left who were in the habit of coming. His dumb, dull presentiment was a prophecy, and his wife's logic was nothing but words.

'Then there are all the rooms here; what shall we do with them?'

'I have told you; you want more space. Besides, you do not make half enough show. You ought to go with the times. Why, at Cross's at Cambridge their upstairs windows are hung full of spades and hoes and such things, and you can see it is business up to the garret. I should turn the parlour into a counting-house. It isn't the proper thing for you to be standing always at that poky little desk at the end of the counter with a pen behind your ear. Turn the parlour, I say, into a counting-house, and come out when Tom finds it necessary to call you. That makes a much better impression. The rooms above the drawing-room might be used for lighter goods, so as not to weight the floors too much.'

Mr Furze was not sentimental, but he shuddered. In the big front bedroom his father and he had been born. The first thing he could remember was having measles there, and watching day by day, when he was a little better, what went on in the street below. His brothers and sisters were also born there. He remembered how his mother was shut up there, and he was not allowed to enter; how, when he tried the door, Nurse Judkins came and said he must be a good boy and go away, and how he heard a little cry, and was told he had a new sister, and he wondered how she got in. In that room his father had died. He was very ill for a long time, and again Nurse Judkins came. He sat up with his father there night after night, and heard the church clock sound all the hours as the sick man lay waiting for his last. He rallied towards the end, and, being very pious, he made his son sit down by the bedside and read to him the ninety-first Psalm. He then blessed his boy in that very room, and five minutes afterwards he had rushed from it, choked with sobbing when the last breath was drawn. He did not relish the thought of taking down the old four-post bedstead and putting rakes and shovels in its place, but all he could say was –

'I don't quite fall in with it.'

'*Why* not? Now, my dear, I will make a bargain with you. If you can assign a good reason, I will give it up; but, if you cannot, then, of course, we ought to go, because *I* have plenty of reasons for going. Nothing can be fairer than that.'

Mr Furze was not quite clear about the 'ought', although it was so fair, but he was mute, and, after a pause, went into his shop. An accident decided the question. Catharine was the lightest sleeper in the house, notwithstanding her youth. Two nights after this controversy she awoke suddenly and smelt something burning. She jumped out of bed, flung her dressing-gown over her, opened her door, and found the landing full of smoke. Without a moment's hesitation she rushed out and roused her parents. They were both bewildered, and hesitated, ejaculating all sorts of useless things. Catharine was impatient.

'Now, then, not a second; upstairs through Jane's bedroom, out into the gutter, and through Hopkins's attic. You cannot go downstairs.'

Still there was trembling and indecision.

'But the tin box,' gasped Mr Furze; 'it is in the wardrobe. I must take it.'

Catharine replied by literally driving them before her. They picked up the maid-servant, crept behind the high parapet, and were soon in safety. By this time the smoke was pouring up thick and fast, although no flame had appeared. Suddenly Catharine cried –

'But where is Tom?'

Tom was the assistant, and slept in an offset at the back. Underneath him was the kitchen, and beyond was the lower offset of the scullery. Catharine darted towards the window.

'Catharine!' shrieked her mother, 'where are you going? You cannot; you are not dressed.'

But she answered not a word, and had vanished before anybody could arrest her. The smoke was worse, and almost suffocating, but she wrapped her face and nose in her woollen gown, and reached Tom's door. He never slept with it fastened, and the amazed youth was awakened by a voice which he knew to be that of Miss Furze. Escape by the way she had come was hopeless. The staircase was not opaque. Fortunately Tom's casement, instead of being in the side wall, was at the end, and the drop to the scullery roof was not above four feet. Catharine reached it easily, and, Tom coming after her, helped her to scramble down into the yard. The gate was unbarred, and in another minute they were safe with their neighbours. The town was now stirring, and a fire-engine came, a machine which attended fires officially, and squirted on them officially, but was never known to do anything more, save to make the road sloppy. The thick, brick party walls of the houses adjoining saved them, but Mr Furze's house was gutted from top to bottom. It was surrounded by a crowd the next day, which stared unceasingly. The fire-engine still operated on the ashes, and a great steam and smother arose. A charred oak beam hung where it had always hung, but the roof had disappeared entirely, and the walls of the old bedchamber, which had seen so much of sweetness and of sadness, of the mysteries of love, birth, and death, lay bare to the sky and the street.

CHAPTER III

The stone bridge was deeply recessed, and in each recess was a
stone seat. In the last recess but one, at the north end, and on the
east side, there sat daily, some few years before 1840, a blind
man, Michael Catchpole by name, selling shoelaces. He orig-
inally came out of Suffolk, but he had lived in Eastthorpe ever
since he was a boy, and had worked for Mr Furze's father. He
was blinded by a splash of melted iron, and was suddenly left
helpless, a widower with one boy, Tom, fifteen years old. His
employer, the present Mr Furze, did nothing for him, save
sending him two bottles of lotion which he had heard were good
for the eyes, and Mike for a time was confounded. His club
helped him so long as he was actually suffering and confined to
his house, but their pay did not last above six weeks. In these six
weeks Mike learned much. He was brought face to face with a
blank wall with the pursuer behind him – an experience which
teaches more than most books, and he was on the point of doing
what some of us have been compelled to do – that is to say, to
recognise that the worst is inevitable, throw up the arms and
bravely yield. But Mike also learned that this is not always
necessary to a man with courage, and that very often escape lies
in the last moment, the very last, when endurance seems no
longer possible. His deliverance did not burst upon him in
rainbow colours out of the sky complete. It was a very slow
affair. He heard that an old woman had died who lived in
Parker's Alley and sold old clothes, old iron, bottles, and such
like trash. Parker's Alley was not very easy to find. Going up
High Street from the bridge, you first turned to the right
through Cross Street, and then to the right again down Lock
Lane, and out of Lock Lane ran the alley, a little narrow gutter
of a place, dark and squalid, paved with round stones, through
which slops of all kinds perpetually percolated, and gave forth

on the cleanest days a faint and sickening odour. Mike thought he could buy the stock for five shillings; the rent was only half a crown a week, and with the help of Tom, a remarkably sharp boy, who could tell him in what condition the goods were which were offered him for purchase, he hoped he could manage to make way. It was a dreadful trial. The old woman had lived amongst all her property. She had eaten and drunk and slept amidst the dirty rags of Eastthorpe, but Mike could not. Fortunately the cottage was at the end of the alley. One window looked out on it, but the door was in a kind of indentation in it round the corner. On the right-hand side of the door was the room looking into the alley, and this Mike made his shop; on the left was a little cupboard of a living-room. He kept the shop window open, so that no customer came through the doorway, and he begged some scarlet geranium cuttings, which, in due time, bloomed into brilliant colour on his sitting-room window-sill, proclaiming that from their possessor hope and delight in life had not departed. Alas! the enterprise was a failure. Mike was no hand at driving hard bargains, and frequently, when the Jew from Cambridge came round to sweep up what Mike had been unable to sell in the town, he found himself the worse for his purchases. The unscalable wall was again in front of him, and his foe at his heels, closer than before, and raging for his blood. He had gone out one morning, Tom leading him, and was passing the bank, when the cashier ran out. Miss Foster, one of the maiden ladies, who it will be remembered, lived in the Abbey Close, had left a sovereign on the counter, and the cashier was exceedingly anxious to show his zeal by promptly returning it, for Miss Foster, it will also be remembered, was a daughter of a former partner in the bank, and still, as it was supposed, retained some interest in it. She had gone too far, however, and the cashier could not venture to leave his post and follow her. Knowing Mike and Tom perfectly well, he asked Mike to take the sovereign at once to the lady. He promptly obeyed, and was in time to restore it to its owner before it was missed. She was not particularly sensitive, but the sight of Mike and Tom standing at the hall entrance rather touched her, and she rewarded them with a shilling. She was also pleased to inquire how Mike was getting on, and he briefly told her he did not get on in any way, save as the most unsuccessful happily get on, and so at last terminate their perplexities. Miss Foster, although well-to-do, kept neither footman nor page, and a thought struck her. She abhorred male servants, but it was very often inconvenient to send her maids on errands. She therefore suggested to Mike that, if he and Tom could station themselves within call, they would not only be useful, but earn something of a livelihood. The bank wanted an odd man occasionally, and she was sure that other people in the town would employ him. Accordingly Mike and Tom one morning established themselves in the recess of the bridge, after having given notice to everybody who would be likely to assist them, and Mike set up a stock of boot-laces and shoe-laces of all kinds. He thus managed to pick up a trifle. He wrapped sacking round his legs to keep off the cold as he sat, and had for a footstool a box with straw in it. He also rigged up a little awning on some sticks to keep off the sun and a shower, but of course when a storm came he was obliged to retreat. He was then allowed a shelter in the bank. The dust was a nuisance, for it was difficult to predict its capricious eddies, but he learnt its laws at last, and how to choose his station so as to diminish annoyance. At first he was depressed at the thought of sitting still for so many hours with nothing to do, but he was not left to himself so much as he anticipated. Two hours on the average were spent on errands; then there was his dinner: Tom talked to him; people went by and said a word or two, and thus he discovered that a foreseen trouble may look impenetrable, but when we near it, or become immersed in it, it is often at least semi-transparent, and even sometimes admits a ray of sunshine. Gradually his employment became sweet to him; he was a part of the town; he heard all its news; it was gentle with him; even the rough boys never molested him; he tamed a black kitten to stay with him, and a red ribbon and a bell were provided for her by a friend. When the kitten grew to be a cat she gravely watched under Mike's awning during his short absences with Tom, and not a soul ever touched the property she guarded. Country folk who came to market on Saturday invariably saluted Mike with their kind

17

country friendliness, and brought him all sorts of little gifts in the shape of fruit, and even of something more substantial when a pig was killed. Thus with Mike time and the hour wore out the roughest day.

Two years had now passed since his accident, and Tom was about seventeen, when Miss Catharine crossed the bridge one fine Monday morning in June with the servant, and, as was her wont stopped to have a word or two with her friend Mike. Mike was always at his best on Monday morning. Sunday was a day of rest, but he preferred Monday. It was a delight to him to hear again the carts and the noise of feet, and to feel that the world was alive once more. Sunday with its enforced quietude and inactivity was a burden to him.

'Well, Miss Catharine, how are you to-day?'

'How did you know I was Miss Catharine? I hadn't spoken.'

'Lord, Miss, I could tell. Though it's only about two years since I lost my eyes, I could tell. I can make out people's footsteps. What a lovely morning! What's going on now down below?'

Mike always took much interest in the wharves by the side of the river.

'Why, Barnes's big lighter is loading malt.'

'Ah! what, the new one with the yellow band round it! that's a beautiful lighter, that is.'

Mike had never seen it.

'What days do you dislike the most? Foggy, damp, dull, dark days?'

These foggy, damp, dull, dark days were particularly distasteful to Catharine.

'No, Miss, I can't say I do, for, you know, I don't see them.'

'Cold, bitter days?'

'They are a bit bad; but somehow I earn more money on cold days than on any other; how it is I don't know.'

'I hate the dust.'

'Ah, now! that *is* unpleasant, but there again, Miss, I dodge it, and it's my belief that it wouldn't worry people half so much if they wouldn't look at it.'

'How much have you earned this morning?'

'Not a penny yet, Miss, but it will come.'

'I want two pairs of shoe-laces,' and Miss Catharine, selecting two pairs, put down a fourpenny-piece, part of her pocket-money, twice the market value of the laces, and tripped over the bridge. When she was at dinner with her father and mother that day she suddenly said –

'Father, didn't Mike Catchpole lose his sight in our foundry?'

'Yes.'

'Have you been talking with him again?' interposed Mrs Furze. 'I wish you would not stop on the bridge as you do. It does not look nice for a girl like you to stay and gossip with Mike.'

Catharine took no notice.

'Did you ever do anything for him?'

'What an odd question!' again interposed Mrs Furze. 'What should we do? There was his club: besides, we sent him the lotion.'

'Why cannot you take Tom as an apprentice?'

'Because,' said her father, 'there is nobody to pay the premium; you know what that means. When a boy is bound apprentice the master has a sum of money for teaching him the business.'

Catharine did not quite comprehend, inasmuch as there were two boys in the back shop who were paid wages, and who were learning their trade. She was quiet for a few minutes, but presently returned to the charge.

'You *must* take Tom. Why shouldn't you give him what you give the other boys?'

'Really, Catharine,' said her mother, 'why *must*?'

'Must!' cried the little miss – 'yes, I say *must*, because Mike lost his eyes for you, and you've done nothing for him; it's a shame.'

'Catharine, Catharine!' said her father, but in accordance with his usual habit he said nothing more, and the mother, also in accordance with her usual habit, collapsed.

Miss Catharine generally, even at that early age, carried all before her, much to her own detriment. Her parents unfortunately were perpetually making a brief show of resistance and afterwards yielding. Frequently they had no pretext for resistance, for Catharine was right and they were wrong. Consequently the child grew up accustomed to see everything bend to her own will, and accustomed to believe that what she willed was in accordance with the will of the universe – not a healthy education, for the time is sure to come when a destiny which will not bend stands in the path before us, and we are convinced by the roughest processes that what we purpose is to a very small extent the purpose of Nature. The shock then is serious, especially if the collision be postponed till mature years. The parental opposition, such as it was, was worse than none, because it enabled her to feel her strength. She continued to press her point, and not only was victorious, but was empowered to tell Mike that his son would be taken into the foundry and paid five shillings and sixpence a week – 'a most special case', as Mr Furze told Mike, in order to stimulate his gratitude.

Mike was now able to find his way about by himself, but before the date of the first chapter in this history he had left the bridge, and Tom supported him.

The morning after the fire beheld the Furze family at breakfast with the hospitable Hopkins. They had saved scarcely any clothes, but Tom and his master were equipped from a ready-made shop. The women had to remain indoors in borrowed garments till they could be made presentable by the dressmaker. Mr Furze was so unfitted to deal with events which did not follow in anticipated, regular order, that he was bewildered. He and Tom went out to look at the ruins, and everything which had to be done seemed to crowd in upon him at once, one thing tumbling incessantly over the other, and nothing staying long enough before him to be settled. Although his business had been fairly large, he had nothing of the faculty of the captain or the manager, who can let details alone and occupy himself with principles. He had a stock of copper bolt-stave in the front shop, and he poked about and pestered the men to know if any of it could be found melted. Then it occurred to him the next instant, and before the inquiry about the bolt-stave could be answered, that he had lost his account-books, and he began to try to recollect what one of his principal customers owed him. Before his memory was fairly exercised on the subject it struck him that the men in the foundry – which was untouched – would not know what to do, and he hurried in, but came out again without leaving any directions. At last he became so confused that he would have broken down if Tom had not come to the rescue, and gently laid hold of his arm.

'Let us go into the Bell;' and into the Bell they went, into the large, empty coffee-room, very quiet at that time of the morning. 'We are better here,' said Tom, 'if we want to know what we ought to do. The first thing is to write to the insurance company.'

'Of course, of course!'

'We will do that at once; I will write the letter, and you sign it.'

In less than ten minutes this stage of the business was passed.

'The next thing is to find a shop while they are rebuilding.'

That was not quite so easy a matter. There was not one in the High Street to be let. At last an idea struck Tom.

'There is the Moot Hall – underneath it, I mean. We shall have to buy fittings, but I will have them so arranged that they will do for the new building. All that is necessary is to obtain leave; but we shall be sure to get it: only half of it is wanted on market days, and that's the part that isn't shut off. We'll then write to Birmingham and Sheffield about the stock. We'd better have a few posters stuck about at once, saying that business will be carried on in the Hall for the present.'

Mr Furze saw the complexity unravel itself, and the knot in his head began to loosen, but he did not quite like to reflect that he owed his relief to Tom, and that Tom had seen his agitation. Accordingly, when a proof of the poster was brought, he was the master, most particularly the master, and observed with much dignity and authority that it ought not to have been set up without the benefit of his revision; that it would not do by any means as it stood, and that it had better be left with him.

Mr and Mrs Hopkins insisted upon continuing their hospitality until a new home could be found, and Mrs Furze urged her project of the Terrace with such eagerness, that at last her husband consented.

'I think,' said Mrs Furze, when the debate was concluded, 'that Catharine had better go away for a short time until we are settled in the Terrace and the shop is rebuilt. She would not be of much use in the new house, and would only knock herself up.'

That was not Mrs Furze's reason. She had said nothing to Catharine, but she instinctively dreaded her hostility to the scheme. Mr Furze knew that was not Mrs Furze's reason, but he accepted it. Mrs Furze knew it was not her own reason, but she also accepted it, and believed it to be the true reason. Such contradictions are quite possible in that mystery of mysteries, the human soul.

'My dear Catharine,' quoth her mother that evening, 'you look worried and done up. No wonder, considering what we have gone through. A change would do you good, and you had better go and stay with your aunt at Ely till we have a roof of our own over our heads once more. She will be delighted to see you.'

Catharine particularly objected to her aunt at Ely. She was a maiden lady and elder sister to Mrs Furze. She had a small annuity, had turned herself into a most faithful churchwoman, and went to live at Ely because it was cheap and a cathedral city. Every day, morning and afternoon, was Aunt Matilda to be seen at the cathedral services, and frequently she was the only attendant, save the choir and officials.

'Why do you want me out of the way?' said Catharine, dismissing without the least notice the alleged pretext.

'I have told you, my dear.'

'I cannot go to Ely. If you wish me to go anywhere, I will go to Mrs Bellamy's.'

'My dear, that is not a sufficient change for you. Ely is a different climate, and I cannot consent to quartering you on a stranger for so long.'

'Mrs Bellamy will not object. Will the new house be like the old one?'

'Well, really, my dear, nothing at present is quite determined; no doubt your father will take the opportunity of making a few improvements.'

'My bedroom, I hope, will be what it was before, and in the

same place.'

'Oh, I – I trust there will be no serious alteration, except what – what will be agreeable to us all, but your father is so much bothered now; perhaps you will have a room which is a little larger, but I really do not know. I cannot say anything; how can you *expect* me to say anything just at present, my dear child?'

Again there was the same contradiction. Mrs Furze knew this was wrong, but she believed it was right. There was, however, a slight balance in favour of what she knew against what she believed, and she hastened to appease her conscience by a mental promise that, as soon as possible, she would tell Catharine that, upon full consideration, they had determined, etc., etc. That would put everything straight morally. Had Catharine put her question yesterday – so Mrs Furze argued – the answer now given would have been perfectly right. She was doing nothing more than giving a reply which was a trifle in arrear of the facts, and, if she rectified it at the earliest date, the impropriety would be nothing. It is sometimes thought that it is those who habitually speak the truth who are most easily deceived. It is not quite so. If the deceivers are not entirely deceived, they profess acquiescence, and perpetual acquiescence induces half-deception. It is, perhaps, more cor- rect to say that the word deception has no particular meaning for them, and implies a standard which is altogether inapplicable. There is a tacit agreement through all society to say things which nobody believes, and that being the constitution under which we live, it is absurd to talk of truth or falsity in the strict sense of the terms. A thing is true when it is in accordance with the system and on a level with it, and false when it is below it. Every now and then at rarest intervals a creature is introduced to us who speaks the veritable reality and wakes in us the slumbering conviction of universal imposture. We know that he is not as other men are; we look into his eyes and see that they penetrate us through and through, but we cannot help ourselves, and we jabber to him as we jabber to the rest of the world. It was ridiculous that her mother should talk as she did to Catharine. Mrs Furze was perfectly aware that she was not deluding her daughter; but she assumed that the delusion was complete.

'Well, mother, I say I cannot go to Ely.'

Catharine again had her own way. She went to Mrs Bellamy's, and Mrs Furze, after having told Mrs Bellamy what was going to happen, begged her not so say anything to Catharine about it.

CHAPTER IV

Mr Bellamy's farm of Westchapel – Chapel Farm it was usually called – lay about half a mile from Lampson's Ford, and about five miles from Eastthorpe. The road from Eastthorpe running westerly and parallel with the river, at a distance of about a mile from it sends out at the fourth milestone a by-road to the south, which crosses the river by a stone bridge, and there is no doubt that before the bridge existed there was a ford, and that there was also a chapel hard by where people probably commended their souls to God before taking the water. In the angle formed by the main road, the lane, and the river, lay Chapel Farm. The house stood on a gentle slope, just enough to lift it above the range of the worst of winter floods, and faced the south. It was not in the lane, but on a kind of private road or cart-track which issued from it; went through a gate and under a hedge; expanded itself in an open space of carefully weeded gravel just opposite the front door, and became a more insignificant and much rougher track on the other side, passing by the stacks into the field, and finally disappearing altogether. From the hand-post on the main road to the gate was half a mile, and from the gate to the farm nearly another half-mile. In driving from Chapel Farm you feel, when you reach the gate, you are in the busy world again, and when you reach the hand-post and turn to Eastthorpe you are in the full tide of life, although not a soul is to be seen. Opposite the house were the farm-buildings and the farmyard. The gate to the right of the farm-buildings led into the meadow, and thus anybody sitting in the front rooms could see the barges slowly and silently towed from the sea to the uplands and back again, the rising ground beyond, and so on to Thingleby, whose little spire just emerged above the horizon. The river, deep and sluggish for the most part, was fringed with willows on the side opposite the towing-path. At the bridge, just where the ford used to be, it was broken into shallows, over which the stream slipped faster, and here and there there were not above two or three feet of water, so that sometimes the barges were almost aground. The farmhouse was not quite ideal. It was plain red brick, now grey and lichen-covered, about a hundred years old; the windows were white-painted, with heavy frames, and the only attempt at ornament was a kind of porch over the front door, supported by brackets, but with no sides to it. Nevertheless, it had its charms. Save on the northern side, where it was backed by the huge elms in the home-field, it lay bare to the winds, breezy, airy, full of light. In summer the front door was always open, and even when it was shut in cold weather no knocker was ever used. If a visitor came by daylight he was always seen, and if after dark he was heard. The garden, which lay on the west side of the house and at the back, was rather warm in hot weather, but was delicious. Under the wall on the north side the apricot and Orleans plum ripened well, and round to the right was the dairy, always cool, sweet, and clean, with the big elder trees before the barred window.

The mistress of the house, Mrs Bellamy, was not a very robust woman. She was generally ailing, but never very seriously ill. She had had two children, but they had both died. Mrs Bellamy's mind, unoccupied with parental cares, with politics, or with literature, let itself loose upon her house, her dairy, and her fowls. She established a series of precautions to prevent dirt, and the precautions themselves became objects to be protected. There was a rough scraper intervening on behalf of the black-leaded scraper; there was a large mat to preserve the mat beyond it and although a drugget covered the stair carpet, Mrs Bellamy would have been sorely vexed if she had found a footmark upon it. If a friend was expected she put some straw outside the garden gate, and she asked him in gentle tones when he dismounted if he would kindly 'just take the worst off' there. The kitchen was scoured and scrubbed till it was fleckless. It was theoretically the living-room, and a defence for the parlour, but it also was defended in its turn like the scraper, and the back kitchen, which had a fireplace, was used for cooking, the fire in the state kitchen not being lighted in summer time. Partly Mrs

Bellamy's excessive neatness was due to the need of an occupation. She brooded much, and the moment she had nothing to do
she became low-spirited and unwell. Partly also it was due to a
touch of poetry. She polished her verses in beeswax and
turpentine, and sought on her floors and tables for that which
the poet seeks in Eden or Atlantis. It must not be imagined that
because she was so particular she was stingy. She was one of the
most open-handed creatures that ever breathed. She loved
plenty. The jug was always full to overflowing with beer, and
the dishes were always heaped up with good things, so that
nobody was ever afraid of robbing his neighbour.

Catharine was never weary of Chapel Farm. She was busy
from morning to night, and the living creatures on it were her
especial delight. Naturally, as is the case with all country girls,
the circumference of her knowledge embraced a region which a
town matron would have veiled from her daughters with the
heaviest curtains.

'How's the foal going on?' said Mrs Bellamy to her husband
one evening when he came in to supper.

'Oh, the foal's all right; he'll be just like his father – just the
same broad hind-quarters. Lord! we shall hardly get him into
the shafts. You remember, Miss Catharine, as I showed you
what extrornary quarters King Tom had when he came here? It
is a curious thing, there ain't one of his foals that hasn't got that
mark of him. I allus likes a horse, I do, that leaves his mark
strong. If you pay pretty heavy you ought to have something for
your money. The mother, though, is in a bad way: my belief is
she'll have milk-fever.'

'That mare never seemed healthy to me,' said Catharine.

'No, she was brought up anyhow. When she was about a
fortnight old her mother died. They didn't know how to manage
her, and half starved her.'

'I don't believe in starvin' creatures when they are young,'
said Mrs Bellamy, who was herself a very small eater.

'Nor I neither, and yet that mare, although, as you say, Miss
Catharine, she was never healthy, has the most wonderful
pluck, as you know. I remember once I had two ton o' muck in
the waggon, and we were struck. Jack and Blossom couldn't stir

it, and, after a bit, chucked up. I put in Maggie – you should have seen her! She moved it, a'most all herself, aye, as far as from here to the gate, and then of course the others took it up. That's blood! What a thing blood is! – you may load it, but you can't break it. Never a touch of the whip would she stand, and yet it's quite true she isn't right, and never was. Maybe the foal will be like her; the shape goes after the father mostly, but the sperrit and temper after the mother.'

The next morning Maggie was worse. Catharine was in the stable as soon as anybody was stirring, and the poor creature was trembling violently. She was watched with the most tender care, and when she became too weak to stand to eat or drink she was slung with soft bands and pads. Her groans were dreadful. After about a week of cruel misery she died. It was evening, and Catharine sat down and looked at what was left of her friend. She had never before even partly realised what death meant. She was too young to feel its full force. The time was yet to come when death would mean despair – when the insolubility of the problem would induce carelessness to all other problems and their solution. Furthermore, this was only a horse. Still, the contrast struck her between the corpse before her and Maggie with her bright eyes and vivid force. What had become of all that strength; what had become of *her*? – and the girl mused, as countless generations had mused before her. Then there was the pathos of it. She thought of the brave animal which she had so often seen, apparently for the mere love of difficulty, struggling as if its sinews would crack. She thought of its glad recognition when she came into the stable, and of its evident affection, half human, or perhaps wholly human, and imprisoned in a form which did not permit full expression. She looked at its body as it lay there extended, quiet, pleading as it were against the doom of man and of beast, and tears came to her eyes as she noted the appeal – tears not altogether of sorrow, but partly of revolt.

Mr Bellamy came in.

'Ah, Miss Catharine, I don't wonder at it. There's many a human as I should less have missed than Maggie. I can't make out at times why we should love the beasts so as perish.'

'Perhaps they don't.'

28

'Really, Miss, of course they do. What's the Lord to do with all the dead horses and cows?'

Catharine thought, 'Or with the dead men and women,' but she said nothing. The subject was new to her. She took her scissors and cut off a wisp of Maggie's beautiful mane, twisted it up, put it carefully in a piece of paper, and placed it in a little pocket-book which she always carried. The next morning as soon as it was daylight a man came over from Eastthorpe; Maggie was hoisted into a cart, her legs dangling down outside, and was driven away to be converted into food for dogs.

One of Catharine's favourite haunts was a meadow by the bridge. She was not given to reading, but she liked a stroll; and, as there were plenty of rats, the dog enjoyed the stroll too. Not a week after Maggie's death she had wandered to this point without her usual companion. A barge had gone down just before she arrived, and for some reason or other had made fast to the bank about a quarter of a mile below her on the side opposite to the towing-path. She sat down under a willow with her face to the water and back to the sun, for it was very hot, and in a few minutes she was half dozing. Suddenly she started, and one of the bargemen stood close by her.

'Hullo, my beauty! Why you was asleep! Wot's the time?'

'I haven't a watch.'

'Haven't a watch! Now that's a shame; if you was mine, my love, you should 'ave one o' gold.'

'It is time I was at home,' said Catharine, rising with as much presence of mind as she could muster; 'and I should think it must be your dinner-hour.'

'Damn my dinner-hour, when I've got the chance of sittin' alongside a gal with sich eyes as yourn, my beauty. Why, you make me all of a tremble. Sit down for a bit.'

Catharine moved away, but the bargee caught her round the waist.

'Sit down, I tell yer, jist for a minute. Who's a-goin' to hurt yer?'

It was of no use to resist, and she did not scream. She sat down, and his arm relaxed its hold to pick up his pipe which had fallen on the other side. Instantly, without a second's hesitation, she leaped up, and, before his heavy bulk could lift itself, she had turned and rushed along the bank. Had she made for the bridge, he would have overtaken her in the lane, but she went the other way. About fifty yards down the stream, and in the direction of Chapel Farm, was a deep hole in the river bed, about five feet wide. On the other side of it there were not more than eighteen inches of water at any point. Catharine knew that hole well, as the haunt of the jack and the perch. She reached it, cleared it at a bound, and alighted on the bit of shingle just beyond it. Her pursuer came up and stared at her silently, with his mouth half open. Just at that moment the distant sound of wheels was heard, and he slowly sauntered back to his barge. Catharine boldly waded over the intervening shallows, and was across just as the cart reached the top of the bridge, but her shoes remained behind her in the mud. It proved to be her father's cart, and to contain Tom, who had been over to Thingleby that morning to see what chance there was of getting any money out of a blacksmith who was largely in Mr Furze's debt. He saw there was something wrong and dismounted.

'Why, Miss Catharine, you are all wet! What is the matter?'

'I slipped down.'

She could not tell the truth, although usually so straight-forward. Tom looked at her inquiringly as if he was not quite sure, but there was something in her face which forbade further investigation.

'You've lost your shoes; you cannot walk home; will you let me give you a lift to Chapel Farm?'

'They do not matter a straw: it is grass nearly the whole way.'

'I'll fish them out, if you will show me where they are.'

'Carried down by this time ever so far.'

'But you will hurt your feet; it isn't all grass; you had better get in.'

She thought suddenly of the barge again, and reflected that the barge might still be moored where it was an hour ago.

'Very well, then, I will go.'

She essayed to put her foot upon the step, but the mud on her stocking was greasy, and she fell backwards. Tom caught her in his arms, and a strange thrill passed through him when he felt that the whole weight of her body rested on him. Many a man there is who can call to mind, across forty years, a silly passage like this in his life. His hair has whitened; all passion ought long ago to have died out of him; thousands of events of infinitely greater consequence have happened; he has read much in philosophy and religion, and has forgotten it all, and a slip on the ice when skating together, or a stumble on the stair, or the pressure of a hand prolonged just for a second in parting, is felt with its original intensity, and the thought of it drives warm blood once more through the arteries.

'Let me get in first,' said Tom, putting some straw on the step.

He got into the cart, and he gently pulled her up, relinquishing her very carefully, and, in fact, not until after his assistance was no longer needed.

'How *did* you manage it?'

'You know how these things happen: it was all over in a minute: how are father and mother?'

'They are very well.'

There was a pause for a minute or two.

'Well, how are things going on at Eastthorpe?'

'Oh, pretty well; the building is three parts done. I don't think, Miss Catharine, you'll ever go back to the old spot again.'

'What do you mean?'

'I don't think your father and mother will leave the Terrace.'

'Very likely,' she replied, decisively. 'It will be better, perhaps, that they should not. I am sure that whatever they do will be quite right.'

'Of course, Miss Catharine, but *I* shall be sorry. I wish my bedroom could have been built up again between the old walls. In that bedroom you saved my life.'

'Rubbish! Even suppose *I* had done it, as you say, I should have done just the same for my silkworms, and then, somehow when I do a thing on a sudden like that, I always feel as if *I* had not done it. I am sure I didn't do it.'

The last few words were spoken in a strangely different tone, much softer and sweeter.

'I don't quite understand.'

31

'I mean,' said Catharine, speaking slowly, as if half surprised at what had occurred to her, and half lost in looking at it – 'I mean that I do not a bit reflect at such times upon what I do. It is as if something or somebody took hold of me, and, before I know where I am, the thing is done, and yet there is no something nor somebody – at least, so far as I can see. It is wonderful, for after all it is I who do it.'

Tom looked intently at her. She seemed to be taking no notice of him and to be talking to herself. He had never seen in that mood before, although he had often seen her abstracted and heedless of what was passing. In a few moments she recovered herself, and the usual every-day accent returned with an added hardness.

'Here we are at Chapel Farm. Mind you say nothing to father or mother; it will only frighten them.'

Mrs Bellamy came to the gate.

'Lor', bless the child! wherever have you been?'

'Slipped into the water and left my shoes behind me, that's all;' and she ran indoors, jumping from mat to mat, and without even so much as bidding Tom good-bye, who rode home, not thinking much about his business, but lost in a muddle of most contradictory presentations, a constant glimmer of Catharine's ankles, wonderment at her accident – was it all true? – the strange look when she disclaimed the honour of his rescue and expounded her philosophy, and the fall between his shoulders. When he slept, his sleep was usually dreamless, but that night he dreamed as he hardly ever dreamed before. He perpetually saw the foot on the step, and she was slipping into his arms continually, until he awoke with the sun.

CHAPTER V

Catharine went home, or rather to the Terrace, soon afterwards, and found that there was no intention of removing to the High Street, although, notwithstanding their three months' probation in the realms of respectability, Mrs Colston had not called, and Mrs Furze was beginning to despair. The separation from the chapel was nearly complete. It had been done by degrees. On wet days Mrs Furze went to church because it was a little nearer, and Mr Furze went to chapel; then Mrs Furze went on fine days, and, after a little interval, Mr Furze went on a fine day. A fund had been set going to 'restore' the church: the heavy roof was to be removed, and a much lighter and handsomer roof covered with slate was to be substituted; the stonework of many of the windows, which the rector declared had begun to show 'signs of incipient decay,' was to be cut out and replaced with new, so as to make, to use the builder's words, 'a good job of it,' and a memorial window was to be put in near the great west window with its stained glass, the Honourable Mr Eaton having determined upon this mode of commemorating the services of his nephew, Lieutenant Eaton, who had died of dysentery in India, brought on by inattention to tropical rules of eating and drinking, particularly the latter. Oliver Cromwell, it was said, had stabled his horses in the church. This, however, is doubtful, for the quantity of stable accommodation he must have required throughout the country, to judge from vergers and guidebooks, must have been much larger than his armies would have needed, if they had been entirely composed of cavalry; and the evidence is not strong that his horses were so ubiquitous. It was further affirmed that, during the Cromwellian occupation, the west window was mutilated; but there was also a tradition that, in the days of George the Third, there were complaints of dinginess and want of light, and that part of the stained glass was removed and sold. Anyhow there was stained glass in the Honourable Mr Eaton's mansion wonderfully like that at East-thorpe. It was now proposed to put new stained glass in the defective lights. Some of the more advanced of the parishioners, including the parson and the builder, thought the old glass had better all come out, 'the only way to make a good job of it'; but at an archidiaconal visitation the archdeacon protested, and he was allowed to have his own way. Then there was the warming, and this was a great difficulty, because no natural exit for the pipe could be found. At last it was settled to have three stoves, one at the west end of the nave, and one in each transept. With regard to the one in the nave there was no help for it but to bore a hole through the wall. The builder undertook 'to give the pipe outside a touch of the Gothic, so that it wouldn't look bad,' and as for the other stoves, there were two windows just handy. By cutting out the head of Matthew in one, and that of Mark in another, the thing was done, and, as Mrs Colston observed, 'the general confused effect remained the same.' There were one or two other improvements, such as pointing all over outside, also strongly recommended by the builder, and the shifting some of the tombs, and repairing the tracery, so that altogether the sum to be raised was considerable. Mrs Colston was one of the collectors, and Mrs Furze called on her after two months' residence in the Terrace, and intimated her wish to subscribe. Mrs Colston took the money very affably, but still she did not return the visit.

Meanwhile Mrs Furze was doing everything she could to make herself genteel. The Terrace contained about a dozen houses; the two in the centre were higher than the rest, and above them, flanked by a large scroll at either end, were the words, 'THE TERRACE,' moulded out of the stucco; up to each door was a flight of stone steps; before each front window on the dining-room floor and the floor above was a balcony protected by cast-iron filigree work, and between each house and the road was a little piece of garden surrounded by a dwarf wall and arrow-head railings. Mrs Furze's old furniture had, nearly all, been discarded or sold, and two new carpets had been bought. The one in the dining-room was yellow and chocolate, and the one upstairs in the drawing-room was a lovely rose-pattern, with large full-blown roses nine inches in diameter in blue vases. The heavy chairs had disappeared, and nice light elegant chairs were bought, insufficient, however, for heavy weights, for one of Mr Furze's affluent customers being brought to the Terrace as a special mark of respect, and sitting down with a flop, as was his wont, smashed the work of art like card-board and went down on the floor with a curse, vowing inwardly never again to set foot in Furze's Folly, as he called it. The pictures, too, were all renewed. The 'Virgin Mary' and 'George the Fourth' went upstairs to the spare bedroom, and some new oleographs, 'a rising art,' Mrs Furze was assured, took their places. They had very large margins, gilt frames, and professed to represent sunsets, sunrises, and full moons, at Tintern, Como, and other places not named, which Mrs Furze, in answer to inquiries, always called 'the Continent.'

Mr Furze had had a longish walk one morning, and was rather tired. When he came home to dinner he found the house upset by one of its periodical cleanings, and consequently dinner was served upstairs, and not in the half-underground breakfast-room, as it was called, which was the real living-room of the family. Mr Furze, being late and weary, prolonged his stay at home till nearly four o'clock, and, notwithstanding a rebuke from Mrs Furze, insisted on smoking his pipe in the dining-room. Presently he took off his coat and put his feet on a chair, Sunday fashion.

'My dear,' said his wife, 'I don't want to interfere with your comfort, but don't you think you might give up that practice of sitting in your shirt sleeves now we have moved?'

'Why because we've moved?' interposed Catharine.

'Catharine, I did not address you; you have no tact, you do not understand.'

'Coat doesn't smell so much of smoke,' replied Mr Furze, giving, of course, any reason but the true reason.

'My dear, if that is the reason, put on another coat, or, better still, buy a proper coat and a smoking-cap. Nothing could be more appropriate than some of those caps we saw at the restoration bazaar.'

'Really, mother, would you like to see father in a velvet jacket and one of those red-tasselled things on his head? I prefer the shirt-sleeves.'

'No doubt you do; you are a Furze, every inch of you.'

There is no saying to what a height the quarrel would have risen if a double knock had not been heard. A charwoman was in the passage with a pail of water and answered the door at once, before she could be cautioned. In an instant she appeared, apron tucked up.

'Mrs Colston, mum,' and in Mrs Colston walked.

Mrs Furze made a dash at her husband's clay pipe, forgetting that its destruction would not make matters better; but she only succeeded in upsetting the chair on which his legs rested, and in the confusion he slipped to the ground.

'Oh, Mrs Colston, I am so sorry you have taken us by surprise; our house is being cleaned; pray walk upstairs – but oh dear, now I recollect the drawing-room is also turned out; what *will* you do, and the smell of the smoke, too!'

'Pray do not disconcert yourself,' replied the brewer's wife, patronisingly; 'I do not mind the smoke, at least for a few minutes.'

Mrs Colston herself had objected strongly to calling on Mrs Furze, but Mr Colston had urged it as a matter of policy, with a view to Mr Furze's contributions to Church revenues.

'I have come purely on a matter of business, Mrs Furze, and will not detain you.'

Mr Furze had retreated into a dark corner, and was putting on his waistcoat with his back to his distinguished guest. Catharine sat at the window quite immovable. Suddenly Mrs Furze bethought herself she ought to introduce her husband and daughter.

'My husband and daughter, Mrs Colston.'

Mr Furze turned half round, put his other arm into his waistcoat, and bowed. He had, of course, spoken to her scores of times in his shop, but he was not supposed to have seen her till that minute. Catharine rose bowed and sat down again.

'Take a chair, Mrs Colston, take a chair,' said Mr Furze, although he had again turned towards the curtain, and was struggling with his coat. Mrs Furze, annoyed that her husband had anticipated her, pulled the easy-chair forward.

'I am afraid I deprived you of your seat,' said the lady, alluding, as Mrs Furze had not the slightest doubt, to his tumble.

'Not a bit, ma'am, not a bit,' and he moved towards Catharine, feeling very uncomfortable, and not knowing what to do with his hands and legs.

'We are so much obliged to you, Mrs Furze, for your subscription to the restoration fund. We find that a new pulpit is much required; the old pulpit, you will remember, is much decayed in parts, and will be out of harmony with the building when it is renovated. Young Mr Cawston, who is being trained as an architect – the builder's son, you know – has prepared a design which is charming, and the ladies wish to make the new pulpit a present solely from themselves.' The smoke got into Mrs Colston's throat, and she coughed. 'We want you, therefore, to help us.'

'With the greatest pleasure.'

'Then how much shall I say? Five pounds?'

'Would you allow me just to look at the subscription list?' interposed Mr Furze, humbly; but before it could be handed to him Mrs Furze had settled the matter.

'Five pounds – oh, yes, certainly, Mrs Colston. Mr Cawston is, I believe, a young man of talent?'

'Undoubtedly, and he deserves encouragement. It must be most gratifying to his father to see his son endeavouring to raise himself from a comparatively humble occupation and surroundings into something demanding ability and education, from a mere trade into a profession.'

Catharine shifted uneasily, raised her eyes, and looked straight at Mrs Colston, but said nothing.

Meanwhile Mr Furze was perusing the list with both elbows on his knees. The difficulty with his hands and legs increased. He was conscious to a most remarkable degree that he had them, and yet they seemed quite foreign members of his body which he could not control.

'Well, ma'am, I think I must be going. I'll bid you good-bye.'

37

'I have finished my errand, Mr Furze, and I must be going too.'

'Oh, pray, do not go yet,' said Mrs Furze, hoping, in the absence of her husband, to establish some further intimacy. Mr Furze shook Mrs Colston's hand with its lemon-coloured glove and departed. Catharine noticed that Mrs Colston looked at the glove – for the ironmonger had left a mark on it – and that she wiped it with her pocket-handkerchief.

'I wish to ask,' said Mrs Furze, in her mad anxiety to secure Mrs Colston, 'if you do not think a new altar-cloth would be acceptable. I should be so happy – I will not say to give one myself, but to undertake the responsibility, and to contribute my share. The old altar-cloth will look rather out of place.'

'Thank you, Mrs Furze; I am sure I can answer at once. It will be most acceptable. You will not, I presume, object to adopting the design of the committee? We will send you a correct pattern. We have thought about the matter for some time, but had at last determined to wait indefinitely on the ground of the expense.'

The expense! Poor Mrs Furze had made her proposal on the spur of the moment. She, in her ignorance, had not thought an altar-cloth a very costly affair, and now she remembered that she had no friends who were not Dissenters. Moreover, to be on the committee was the object of her ambition, and it was clear that not only had nobody thought of putting her on it, but that she was to pay to take its directions.

'I believe,' continued Mrs Colston, 'that the altar-cloth which we had provisionally adopted can be had in London for £20.'

A ring at the front bell during this interesting conversation had not been noticed. The charwoman, still busy with broom and pail outside, knocked at the door with a knock which might have been given with the broom-handle and announced another visitor.

'Mrs Bellamy, mum.'

Catharine leaped up, rushed to meet her friend, caught her round the neck, and kissed her eagerly.

'Well, Miss Catharine, glad to see you looking so well; still kept the colour of Chapel Farm. This is the first time I've seen you in your new house, Mrs Furze. I had to come over to Eastthorpe along with Bellamy, and I said I *must* go and see my Catharine, though – and her mother – though they *do* live in the Terrace, but I couldn't get Bellamy to come – no, he said the Terrace warn't for him; he'd go and smoke a pipe and have something to drink at your old shop, or rather your new shop, but it's in the old place in the High Streeet – leastways if you keep any baccy and whiskey there now – and he'd call for me with the gig, and I said as I knew my Catharine – her mother – would give me a cup of tea; and, Miss Catharine, you remember that big white hog as you used to look at always when you went out into the meadow? – well, he's killed, and I know Mr Furze likes a bit of good, honest, country pork – none of your nasty town-fed stuff – you never know what hogs eat in towns – so Bellamy has a leg about fourteen pounds in the gig, but I thought I'd bring you about two or three pounds of the sausages in myself in my basket here,' and Mrs Bellamy pointed to a basket she had on her arm. She paused and became aware that there was a stranger sitting near the fireplace. 'But you've got a visitor here; p'r'aps I shall be in the way.'

'In the way!' said Catharine. 'Never, never; give me your basket and your bonnet; or stay, Mrs Bellamy, I will go upstairs with you, and you shall take off your things.'

And so, before Mrs Furze had spoken a syllable, Catharine and Mrs Bellamy marched out of the room.

'Who is that – that person?' said Mrs Colston. 'I fancy I have seen her before. She seems on intimate terms with your daughter.'

'She is a farmer's wife, of humble origin, at whose house my daughter – lodged – for the benefit of her health.'

'I must bid you good-day, Mrs Furze. If you will kindly send a cheque for the five pounds to me, the receipt shall be returned to you in due course, and the drawing of the altar-cloth shall follow. I can assure you of the committee's thanks.'

Mrs Furze recollected she ought to ring the bell but she also recollected the servant could not appear in proper costume. Accordingly she opened the dining-room door herself.

'Let me move that 'ere pail, mum, or you'll tumble over it,' said the charwoman to Mrs Colston, 'and p'r'aps you won't mind steppin' on this side of the passage, 'cause that side's all wet. 'Ere, Mrs Furze, don't you come no further, I'll open the front door;' and this she did.

Mrs Furze felt rather unwell, and went to her bedroom, where she sat down, and, putting her face on the bedclothes, gave way to a long fit of hysterical sobbing. She would not come down to tea, and excused herself on the ground of sickness. Catharine went up to her mother and inquired what was the matter, but was repulsed.

'Nothing is the matter – at least, nothing you can understand. I am very unwell; I am better alone; go down to Mrs Bellamy.'

'But, mother, it will do you good to be downstairs. Mrs Bellamy will be so glad to see you, and she was so kind to me; it will be odd if you don't come.'

'Go *away*, I tell you; I am best by myself; I can endure in solitude; you cannot comprehend these nervous attacks, happily for you; go *away* and enjoy yourself with Mrs Bellamy and your sausages.'

Catharine had had some experience of these nervous attacks, and left her mother to herself. Mrs Bellamy and Catharine consequently had tea alone, Mr Furze remaining at his shop that afternoon, as he had been late in arrival.

'Sorry mother's so poorly, Catharine. Well, how do you like the Terrace?'

'I hate it. I detest every atom of the filthy, stuck-up, stuccoed hovel. I hate – ' Catharine was very excited, and it is not easy to tell what she might have said if Mrs Bellamy had not interrupted her.

'Now, Miss Catharine, don't say that; it's a bad thing to hate what we must put up with. You never heard, did you, as Bellamy had a sister a good bit older than myself? She *was* a tartar, and no mistake. She lived with Bellamy and kept house for him, and when we married, Bellamy said she must stay with us. She used to put on him as you never saw, but he, somehow, seemed never to mind it; some men don't feel such things, and some do, but most on 'em don't when it's a woman, but I think a woman's worse. Well, what was I saying? – she put on me just in the same way and come between me and the servant-girl and the men, and when I told them to go and do one thing, went and told them to do another, and I was young, and I thought when I was married I was going to be mistress, and she called me 'a chit' to her brother, and I mind one day I went upstairs and fell on my knees and cried till I thought my heart would break, and I said, "O my God, when will it please Thee to take that woman to Thyself?" Now to wish anybody dead is bad enough, but to ask the Lord to take 'em is awful; but then it was so hard to bear 'cause I couldn't say nothing about it, and I'm one of them as can't keep myself bottled up like gingerbeer. You don't remember old Jacob? He had been at Chapel Farm in Bellamy's father's time, and always looked on Bellamy as his boy, and used to be very free with him, notwithstanding he was the best creature as ever lived. He took a liking to me, and I needn't say that, liking of me, he didn't like Bellamy's sister. Well, I came down, and I went out of doors to get a bit of fresh air – for I'm always better out of doors – and I went up by the cart-shed, and being faint a bit, sat down on the waggon shafts. Old Jacob, he came by; I can see him now; it was just about Michaelmas time, a-getting dark after tea, though I hadn't had any, and he said to me, "Hullo, missus, what are you here for? and you've been a-cryin'," for I had my face toward the sky and was looking at it. I never spoke. "I know what's the matter with you," says he; "do you think I don't? Now if you go on chafing of yourself, you'll worrit yourself into your grave, that's all. Last week there was something the matter with that there dog, and she howled night after night, and I never slept a wink. The first morning after she'd been a-yelping I was in a temper, and had half a mind to kill her. I felt as if she'd got a spite against me; but it come to me as she'd got no spite against *me*, and then all my worriting went away. I don't say as I slept much till she was better, but I didn't *worrit*. Now Bellamy's sister don't mean nothing against you. That's the way God-a-mighty made her." I've never forgot what Jacob said, and I know it made a difference, but the Lord took her not long afterwards.'

'But I don't see what that has to do with me. It isn't the same thing.'

'Yes, that's just what Bellamy says. He says I always go on with anything that comes into my head; but then it has nothing to do with anything he is saying, and maybe that's true, for one thing seems always to draw me on to another, and so I go round like, and I don't know myself where I am when I've finished. A little more tea, my dear, if you please. And yet,' continued Mrs Bellamy, when she had finished half of her third cup, 'what I meant to say really has to do with you. It's all the same. You wouldn't hate the Terrace so much if you knew that nobody meant to spite you, as Jacob said. Suppose your father was driven to the Terrace and couldn't help it, and there wasn't another house for him, you wouldn't hate it so much then. It isn't the Terrace altogether. Now, Miss Catharine, you won't mind my speaking out to you. You know you are my girl,' and Mrs Bellamy turned and kissed her; 'you mustn't, you really mustn't. I've seen what was coming for a long time. Your mother and you ain't alike, but you mustn't rebel. I'm a silly old fool, and I know I haven't got a head, and what is in it is all mixed up somehow, but you'll be ever so much better if you leave your mother out of it, and don't, as I've told you before, go on dreaming she came here because you didn't want to come, or that she set herself up on purpose against you. And then you can always run over to Chapel Farm just whenever you like, my pet, and there's your own room always waiting for you.'

An hour afterwards, when Mrs Bellamy had left, Mr Furze came home. Mrs Furze was still upstairs, but consented to be coaxed down to supper. She passed the drawing-room; the door was wide open, and she reflected bitterly upon the new carpet, the oleographs, and the schemes erected thereon. To think on what she had spent and what she had done, and then that Mrs Colston should be received by a charwoman with a pail should be shown into the room downstairs, and find it like a public-house bar! If Mr Furze had been there alone it would not so much have mattered, but the presence of wife and daughter sanctioned the vulgarity, not to say indecency. Mrs Colston would naturally conclude they were accustomed to that sort of thing – that the pipe, Mrs Bellamy and the sausages, the absence of Mr Furze's coat and waistcoat, were the 'atmosphere,' as Mrs

Furze put it, in which they lived.

'That's right; glad to see you are able to come down,' said Mr Furze.

'I must say that Catharine is partly the cause of my suffering. When Mrs Colston called here Catharine sat like a statue and said not a word, but when her friend Mrs Bellamy came she precipitated herself – yes, I say precipitated herself – into her arms. I've nothing to say against Mrs Bellamy, but Catharine knows perfectly well that Mrs Colston's intimacy is desired, and *that's* the way she chose to behave. Mrs Bellamy was the last person I should have wished to see here this afternoon; an uneducated woman, a woman whom we could not pretend to know if we moved in Mrs Colston's circle; and what we have done was all done for my child's benefit. She, I presume, would prefer decent society to that of peasants.'

Catharine stopped eating.

'Mrs Bellamy was the last person *I* should have wished to see here.'

'I don't know quite what you mean, but it is probably something disobedient and cruel,' and Mrs Furze became slightly hysterical again.

Catharine made no offer of any sympathy, but, leaving her supper unfinished, rose without saying good-night, and appeared no more that evening.

CHAPTER VI

'My dear,' said Mrs Furze to her husband the next night when they were alone, 'I think Catharine would be much better if she were sent away from home for a time. Her education is very imperfect, and there are establishments where young ladies are taken at her age and finished. It would do her a world of good.'

Mr Furze was not quite sure about the finishing. It savoured of a region outside the modest enclosure within which he was born and brought up.

'The expense, I am afraid, will be great, and I cannot afford it just now. There is no denying that business is no better; in fact, it is not so good as it was, notwithstanding the alterations.'

'You cannot expect it to recover at once. Something must be done to put Catharine on a level with the young women in her position and my notion is that everything which will help to introduce us into society will help you. Why does Mrs Butcher go out so much? It is because she knows it is a good investment.'

'An ironmonger is not a doctor.'

'Who said he was?' replied Mrs Furze, triumphant in the consciousness of mental superiority. 'Furze,' she once said to him, when it was proposed to elect him a guardian of the poor, 'take my advice and refuse. Your *forte* is not argument: you will never hold your own in debate.'

'I know an ironmonger is not a doctor,' she continued; '*I* of all people have reason to know it; but what I do say is, that the more we mix with superior people, the more likely you are to succeed, and that if you bury yourself in these days you will fail.'

The italicised 'I' was an allusion to a fiction that once Mrs Furze might have married a doctor if she had liked, and thereby have secured the pre-eminence which the wife of a drug-dispenser assumes in a country town. The grades in Eastthorpe were very marked, and no caste distinctions could have been

44

more rigid. The country folk near were by themselves. They associated with none of the townsfolk, save with the rector, and even in that relationship there was a slight tinge of ex-officiosity. Next to the rector were the lawyer and the banker and the two maiden banker ladies in the Abbey Close. Looked at from a distance these might be supposed to stand level but, on nearer approach, a difference was discernible. The banker and the ladies, although they visited the lawyer, were a shade beyond him. Then came the brewer. The days had not arrived when brewing – at least, on the large scale – is considered to be more respectable than a learned profession, and Mrs Colston, notwithstanding her wealth, was incessantly forced by the lawyer's wife to confess subordination. The brewer kept three or four horses for pleasure, and the lawyer kept only one; but 'Colston's Entire' was on a dozen boards in the town, and he supplied private families and sent in bills. The position of Mrs Butcher was perhaps the most curious. She visited the rector, banker, lawyer, and brewer, and was always well received, for she was clever, smart, young, and well behaved. She had established her position solely by her wits. She did not spend a quarter as much as Mrs Colston, but she always looked better. She was well shaped, to begin with, and the fit of her garments was perfect. Not a wrinkle was to be seen in gown, gloves, or shoes. Mrs Colston's fashion was that imposed on her by the dressmaker, but Mrs Butcher always had a style peculiarly her own. She knew the secret that a woman's attractiveness, so far as it is a matter of clothes, depends far more upon the manner in which they are made and worn than upon costliness. It was always thought that she ruled her husband and had just a spice of contempt for him. She gained thereby in Eastthorpe, at least with the men, for her superiority to him gave her an air which was slightly detached, free, and fascinating. She always drove when she went out with him, and it was really a sight worth seeing: she bolt upright with her hands well down, her pretty figure showing to the best advantage the neat turn-out – for she was very particular on this point and understood horses thoroughly – and Butcher leaning back, submissive but satisfied. She had made friends with the women too. She was much too shrewd to incur their hostility by openly courting the admiration of their husbands. She knew they did admire her, and that was enough. She was most deferential to Mrs Colston, so much so that the brewer's wife openly expressed the opinion that she was evidently well bred, and wondered how Butcher managed to secure her. Furthermore she was useful, for her opinion, when anything had to be done, was always the one to be followed, and without her the church restoration would never have been such a success. Eastthorpe, like Mrs Colston, often marvelled that Butcher should have been so fortunate. It mostly knew everything about the antecedents of everybody in the town, but Mrs Butcher's were not so well known. She came from Cornwall, she always said, and Cornwall was a long way off in those days. Her maiden name was Treherne, and Mrs Colston had been told that Treherne was good Cornish. Moreover, soon after the marriage, she found on the table, when she called on Mrs Butcher, a letter which she could not help partly reading, for it lay wide open. All scruples were at once removed. It had a crest at the top, was dated from Helston, addressed Mrs Butcher by a nickname, and was written in a most aristocratic hand – so Mrs Colston averred to her intimate friends. She could not finish the perusal before Mrs Butcher came into the room; but she had read enough, and the doctor's elect was admitted at once without reservation. Eastthorpe was slightly mistaken, but Mrs Butcher's history cannot be told here.

So much by way of digression on Eastthorpe society.

Mrs Furze carried her point as usual. As for Catharine, she did not object, for there was nothing in Eastthorpe attractive to her. The Limes, Abchurch, was the 'establishment' chosen. It was kept by the Misses Ponsonby, Abchurch being a large village five miles further eastward. It was a peculiar institution. It was a school for girls, but not for little girls, and it was also an educational home for young ladies up to one- or two-and-twenty whose training had been neglected or had to be completed beyond the usual limits. It was widely known, and, as its purpose was special, it had little or no competition, and consequently flourished. Many parents who had become wealthy, and who hardly knew the manners and customs of the class to which they aspired, sent their daughters to the Limes. The Misses Ponsonby – Miss Ponsonby and Miss Adela Ponsonby – were of Irish extraction, and had some dim connection with the family of that name. They also preserved in their Calvinistic evangelicalism a trace of the Cromwellian Ponsonby, the founder of the race. There was a difference of two years in the age of the two ladies, but no perceptible difference in their characters. The same necessity to conceal or suppress all individuality on subjects disputable in their own sect had been imposed on each. Both had the same 'views' on all matters religious and social, and both of them confessed that on many points their 'views' were 'strict' – whatever that singular phrase may have meant. Nevertheless, they displayed remarkable tact in reconciling parents with the defects and peculiarities of their children. There were always girls in the school of varying degrees of intelligence, from absolute stupidity to brilliancy, but the report at the end of the term was so fashioned that the father and mother of the idiot were not offended, and the idiocy was so handled that it appeared to have some advantages. If Miss Carter had been altogether unable to master the French verbs, or to draw the model vase until the teacher had put in nearly the whole of the outline, there was a most happy counterpoise, as a rule, in her moral conduct. In these days of effusive expression, when everybody thinks it his duty to deliver himself of everything in him – doubts, fears, passions – no matter whether he does harm thereby or good, the Misses Ponsonby would be considered intolerably dull and limited. They did not walk about without their clothes – figuratively speaking – it was not then the fashion. They were, on the contrary, heavily draped from head to foot, but underneath the whalebone and padding, strange to say, were real live women's hearts. They knew what it was to hope and despair; they knew what it was to reflect that with each of them life might and ought to have been different; they even knew what it was sometimes to envy the beggar-woman on the doorstep of the Limes who asked for a penny and clasped a child to her breast. We mistake our ancestors who read Pope and the *Spectator*. They were very much like ourselves essentially, but

47

they did not believe that there was nothing in us which should be smothered or strangled. Perhaps some day we shall go back to them, and find that the 'Rape of the Lock' is better worth reading and really more helpful than magazine metaphysics. Anyhow, it is certain that the training which the Misses Ponsonby had received, although it may have made them starched, prim, and even uninteresting, had an effect upon their character not altogether unwholesome, and prevented any public crying for the moon, or any public charge of injustice against its Maker because it is unattainable.

The number of girls was limited to thirty. The house was tall, four-square, built of white brick about the year 1780, had a row of little pillars running along the roof at the top, and a Grecian portico. It was odd that there should be such a house in Abchurch, but there it was. It was erected by a Spitalfields silk manufacturer, whose family belonged to those parts. He thought to live in it after his retirement, but he came there to die. The studies of the pupils were superintended by the Misses Ponsonby and sundry teachers, all female, except the drawing-master and the music-master. The course embraced the usual branches of a superior English education, French, Italian, deportment, and the use of the globes, but, as the Misses Ponsonby truly stated in their prospectus, their sole aim was not the inculcation of knowledge, but such instruction as would enable the young ladies committed to their charge to move with ease in the best society, and, above everything, the impression of correct principles in morality and religion. In this impression much assistance was given by the Reverend Theophilus Cardew, the rector of the church in the village. The patronage was in the hands of the Simeonite trustees, and had been bought by them in the first fervour of the movement.

The thirty pupils occupied fifteen bedrooms, although each had a separate bed, and to Catharine was allotted Miss Julia Arden, a young woman with a pretty, pale face, and black hair worn in ringlets. Her head was not firmly fixed on her shoulders, and was always in motion, as if she had some difficulty in balancing it, the reason being, not any physical defect, but a wandering imagination, which never permitted her to look at any one thing steadily for an instant. Nine-tenths of what she said was nonsense, but her very shallowness gave occasionally a certain value and reality to her talk, for the simple reason that she was incapable of the effort necessary to conceal what she thought for the moment. In her studies she made not the slightest progress, for her memory was shocking. She confounded all she was taught, and never could recollect whether the verb was conjugated and the noun declined, or whether it was the other way round, to use one of her favourite expressions, so that her preceptors were compelled to fall back, more exclusively than with her schoolfellows, on her moral conduct, which was outwardly respectable enough, but by the occupant of the other bed might perhaps have been reported on in terms not quite so satisfactory as those in the quarterly form signed by Miss Ponsonby.

Catharine's mother came with her on a Saturday afternoon, but left in the evening. At half-past eight there were prayers. The girls filed into the drawing-room, sat round in a ring, of which the Misses Ponsonby formed a part, but with a break of about two feet right and left, the servants sitting outside near the door: a chapter was read, a prayer also read, and then, after a suitable pause, the servants rose from their knees, the pupils rose next, and the Misses Ponsonby last; the time which each division, servants, pupils, and Ponsonbys remained kneeling being graduated exactly in proportion to rank. A procession to the supper-room was then formed. Catharine found herself at table next to Miss Arden, with a spotless napkin before her, with silver forks and spoons, and a delicately served meal of stewed fruits, milk-puddings, bread-and-butter, and cold water. Everything was good, sweet, and beautifully clean, and there was enough. At half-past nine in accordance with the usual practice, one of the girls read from a selected book. On Saturday a book, not exactly religious, but related to religion as nearly as possible as Saturday is related to Sunday, was invariably selected. On this particular Saturday it was Clarke's 'Travels in Palestine.' Precisely as the clock struck ten the volume was closed and the pupils went to bed.

'I am sure I shall like you,' observed Miss Arden, as they were

49

undressing. 'The girl who was here before was a brute, so dull and so vulgar. I hope you will like me.'

'I hope so too.'

'It's dreadful here: so different to my mother's house in Devonshire. We have a large place there near Torquay – do you know Torquay? And I have a horse of my own, on which I tear about during the holidays, and there are boats and sailing matches, and my brothers have so many friends, and I have all sorts of little affairs. I suppose you've had your affairs. Of course you won't say. We never see a man here, except Mr Cardew. Oh, isn't he handsome? He's only a parson, but he's such a dear; you'll see him to-morrow. I can't make him out: he's lovely, but he's queer, so solemn at times, like an owl in daylight. I'm sure he's well brought up. I wonder why he went into the church: he ought to have been a gentleman.'

'But is he not a gentleman?'

'Oh, yes, of course he's a gentleman, but you know what I mean.'

'No, I don't.'

'There, now, you are one of those horrid creatures, I know you are, who never *will* understand, and do it on purpose. It is so aggravating.'

'Well, but you said he was not a gentleman, and yet that he was a gentleman.'

'You *are* provoking. I say he is a gentleman – but don't some gentlemen keep a carriage? – and his father is in business. Isn't that plain? You know all about it as well as I do.'

'I still do not quite comprehend.'

Catharine took a little pleasure in forcing people to be definite, and Miss Arden invariably fell back on 'you understand' whenever she herself did not understand. In fact, in exact proportion to her own inability to make herself clear to herself, did she always insist that she was clear to other people.

'I cannot help it if you don't comprehend. He's lovely, and I adore him.'

Next morning, being Sunday, the Limes was, if possible, still more irreproachable; the noise of the household was more subdued; the passions appeared more utterly extinguished, and any indifferent observer would have said that from the Misses Ponsonby down to the scullery-maid, a big jug had been emptied on every spark of illegal fire, and blood was toast and water. Alas! it was not so. The boots were cleaned overnight to avoid Sunday labour, but when the milkman came, a handsome young fellow, anybody with ears near the window overhead might have detected a scuffling at the back door with some laughter and something like 'Oh, don't!' and might have noticed that Elizabeth afterwards looked a little rumpled and adjusted her cap. Nor was she singular, for many of the young women who were supposed to be studying a brief abstract of the history of the kingdoms of Judah and Israel, in parallel columns, as arranged by the Misses Ponsonby, were indulging in the naughtiest thoughts and using naughty words as they sat in their bedrooms before the time for departure to church. At a quarter-past ten the girls assembled in the dining-room, and were duly marshalled. They did not, however, walk two-and-two like ordinary schools. In the first place, many of them were not children, and, in the second place, the Misses Ponsonby held that even walking to church was a thing to be taught, and they desired to turn out their pupils so that they might distinguish themselves in this art also as well-bred people. It was one of the points on which the Misses Ponsonby grew even eloquent. How, they said, are girls to learn to carry themselves properly if they march in couples? They will not do it when they leave the Limes, and will be utterly at fault. There is no day in the week on which more general notice is taken than on Sunday; there is no day on which differences are more apparent. The pupils therefore walked irregularly, the irregularity being prescribed. The entering the church; the leaving the pews; the loitering and salutations in the churchyard; the slow, superior saunter homewards were all the result of lecture, study, and even of practice on week-days. 'Deliberation, ease,' said Miss Ponsonby, 'are the key to this, as they are to so much in our behaviour, and surely on the Sabbath we ought more than on any other day to avoid indecorous hurry and vulgarity.'

Catharine's curiosity, after what Miss Arden had said, was a little excited to know what kind of a man Mr Cardew might be, and she imagined him a young dandy. She saw a man about thirty-five with dark brown hair, eyes set rather deeply in his head, a little too close together, a delicate, thin, very slightly aquiline nose, and a mouth with curved lips, which were, however, compressed as if with determination or downright resolution. There was not a trace of dandyism in him, and he reminded her immediately of a portrait she had seen of Edward Irving in a shop at Eastthorpe.

He stood straight up in the pulpit reading from a little Testament he held in his hand, and when he had given out his text he put the Testament down and preached without notes. His subject was a passage in the life of Jesus taken from Luke xviii. 18:–

18. *And a certain ruler asked Him, saying, Good Master, what shall I do to inherit eternal life?*

19. *And Jesus said unto him, Why callest thou Me good? None is good, save one, that is God.*

20. *Thou knowest the commandments, Do not commit adultery, Do not kill, Do not steal, Do not bear false witness, Honour thy father and mother.*

21. *And he said, All these have I kept from my youth up.*

22. *Now when Jesus heard these things, He said unto him, Yet lackest thou one thing: sell all that thou hast and distribute unto the poor, and thou shalt have treasure in heaven: and come, follow Me.*

Mr Cardew did not approach his theme circuitously or indifferently, but seemed in haste to be on close terms with it, as if it had dwelt with him and he was eager to deliver his message.

'I beseech you,' he began, 'endeavour to make this scene real to you. A rich man, an official, comes to Jesus, calls Him Teacher – for so the word is in the Greek – and asks Him what is to be done to inherit eternal life. How strange it is that such a question should be so put! how rare are the occasions on which two people approach one another so nearly! Most of us pass days, weeks, months, years in intercourse with one another, and nothing which even remotely concerns the soul is ever mentioned. Is it that we do not care? Mainly that, and partly because we foolishly hang back from any conversation on what it is most important we should reveal, so that others may help us. Whenever you feel any promptings to speak of the soul or to make any inquiries on its behalf, remember it is a sacred duty not to suppress them.

'This ruler was happy in being able to find a single authority to whom he could appeal for an answer. If anybody wishes for such answer now, he can find no oracle sole and decisive. The voices of the Church, the sects, the philosophers are clamorous but discordant, and we are bewildered. And yet, as I have told you over and over again in this pulpit, it is absolutely necessary that you should have one and one only supreme guide. To say nothing of eternal salvation, we must, in the conduct of life, shape our behaviour by some one standard, or the result is chaos. We must have some one method or principle which is to settle beforehand how we are to do this or that, and the method or principle should be Christ. Leaving out of sight altogether His Divinity, here is no temper, no manner so effectual, so happy as His for handling all human experience. Oh, what a privilege it is to meet with anybody who is controlled into unity, whose actions are all directed by one consistent force!

'Jesus, as if to draw from this ruler all that he himself believed, tells him to keep the Law. The Law, however, is insufficient, and it is noteworthy that the ruler felt it to be so. To begin with it is largely negative: there are three negatives in this twentieth verse for one affirmative, and negations cannot redeem us. The law is also external. As a proof that it is ineffectual, I ask, Have you ever *rejoiced* in it? Have you ever been kindled by it? Have all its precepts ever moved you like one single item in the story of the love of Jesus? Is the man attractive to you who has kept the law and done nothing more? Would not the poor woman who anointed our Lord's feet and wiped them with her hair be more welcome to you than the holy people who had simply never transgressed?

'We are struck with the magnitude of the demand made by Jesus on this ruler. To obtain eternal life he was to sell all he had, give up house, friends, position, respectability, and lead a vagrant life in Palestine with this poor carpenter's son. Alas! eternal life is not to be bought on lower terms. Beware of the damnable doctrine that it is easy to enter the kingdom of heaven. It is to be obtained only by the sacrifice of *all* that stands in the way, and it is to be observed that in this, as in other things, men will take the first, the second, the third – nay, even the ninety-ninth step, but the hundredth and last they will not take. Do you really wish to save your soul? Then the surrender must be absolute. What! you will say, am I to sell everything? If Christ comes to you – *yes*. Sell not only your property, but your very self. Part with all your preferences, your loves, your thoughts, your very soul, if only you can gain Him, and be sure too that He will come to you in a shape in which it will not be easy to recognise Him. What a bargain, though, this ruler would have made! He would have given up his dull mansion in Jerusalem, Jerusalem society, which cared nothing for *him*, though it doubtless called on him, made much of him, and even professed undying friendship with him; he would have given this up, nothing but this, and he would have gained those walks with Jesus across the fields, and would have heard Him say, "Consider the lilies!" "Oh, yes, we would have done it at once!" we cry. I think not, for Christ is with us even now.'

Curiously enough, the conclusion was a piece of the most commonplace orthodoxy, lugged in, Heaven knows how, and delivered monotonously, in strong contrast to the former part of the discourse. – M. R.

These notes, made by one who was present, are the mere ashes, cold and grey, of what was once a fire. Mr Cardew was really eloquent, and consequently a large part of the effect of what he said is not to be reproduced. It is a pity that no record is possible of a great speaker. The writer of this history remembers when it was his privilege to listen continually to a man whose power over his audience was so great that he could sway them unanimously by a passion which was sufficient for any heroic deed. The noblest resolutions were formed under that burning oratory, and were kept, too, for the voice of the dead preacher still vibrates in the ears of those who heard him. And yet, except in their hearts, no trace abides, and when they are dead he will be forgotten, excepting in so far as that which has once lived can never die.

Whether it was the preacher's personality, or what he said, Catharine could hardly distinguish, but she was profoundly moved. Such speaking was altogether new to her; the world in which Mr Cardew moved was one which she had never entered, and yet it seemed to her as if something necessary and familiar to her, but long lost, had been restored. She began now to look forward to Sunday with intense expectation; a new motive for life was supplied to her, and a new force urged her through each day. It was with her as we can imagine it to be with some bud long folded in darkness which, silently in the dewy May night, loosens its leaves, and, as the sun rises, bares itself to the depths of its cup to the blue sky and the light.

CHAPTER VII

The Misses Ponsonby speedily came to a conclusion about
Catharine, and she was forthwith labelled as a young lady of
natural ability, whose education had been neglected, a type
perfectly familiar, recurring every quarter, and one with which
they were perfectly well able to deal. All the examples they had
had before were ticketed in exactly the same terms, and, so
classed, there was an end of further distinction. The means
taken with Catharine were those which had been taken since the
school began, and special attention was devoted to the branches
in which she was most deficient, and which she disliked. Her
history was deplorable, and her first task, therefore was what
were called dates. A table had been prepared of the kings and
queens of England – when they came to the throne, and when
they died; and another table gave the years of all the battles. A
third table gave the relationship of the kings and queens to each
other, and the reasons for succession. All this had to be learned
by heart. In languages, also, Catharine was singularly defective.
Her French was intolerable and most inaccurate, and of Italian
she knew nothing. Her dancing and deportment were so 'provincial,' as Miss Adela Ponsonby happily put it, that it was
thought better that the dancing and deportment teacher should
give her a few private lessons before putting her in a class, and
she was consequently instructed alone in the rudiments of the
art of entering and leaving a room with propriety, of sitting with
propriety on a sofa when conversing, of reading a book in a
drawing-room, of acknowledging an introduction, of sitting
down to a meal and rising therefrom, and in the use of the
pocket-handkerchief. She had particularly shocked the Misses
Ponsonby on this latter point, as she was in the habit of blowing
her nose energetically, 'snorting,' as one of the young ladies said
colloquially, but with truth, and the deportment mistress had

some difficulty in reducing her to the whisper, which was all that was permitted in the Ponsonby establishment, even in cases of severe cold. On the other hand, in one or two departments she was far ahead of the other girls, particularly in arithmetic and geometry.

It was the practice on Monday morning for the girls to be questioned on the sermons of the preceding Sunday, and a very solemn business it was. The whole school was assembled in the big schoolroom, and Mr Cardew, both the Misses Ponsonby being present, examined *viva voce*. One Monday morning, after Catharine had been a month at the school, Mr Cardew came as usual. He had been preaching the Sunday before on a favourite theme, and his text had been, 'So then with the mind I myself serve the law of God, but with the flesh the law of sin,' and the examination at the beginning was in the biography of St Paul, as this had formed a part of his discourse. No fault was to be found with the answers on this portion of the subject, but presently the class was in some difficulty.

'Can anybody tell me what meaning was assigned to the phrase, "The body of this death"?'

No reply.

'Come, you took notes, and one or two interpretations were discarded for that which seemed to be more in accordance with the mind of St Paul. Miss Arden' – Miss Arden was sitting nearest to Mr Cardew – 'cannot you say?'

Miss Arden shook her ringlets, smiled, and turned a little red, as if she had been complimented by Mr Cardew's inquiries after the body of death and glancing at her paper, replied –

'The death of this body.'

'Pardon me, that was one of the interpretations rejected.'

'This body of death,' said Catharine.

'Quite so.'

Mr Cardew turned hastily round to the new pupil, whom he had not noticed before, and looked at her steadily for a moment.

'Can you proceed a little and explain what that means?'

Catharine's voice trembled, but she managed to read from her paper: 'It is strikingly after the manner of St Paul. He opposes the two natures in him by the strongest words at his command –

death and life. One *is* death, the other *is* life, and he prays to be delivered from death; not the death of the body, but from death-in-life.'

'Thank you; that is very nearly what I intended.'

Mr Cardew took tea at the Limes about once a fortnight with Mrs Cardew. The meal was served in the Misses Ponsonby's private room, and the girls were invited in turn. About a fortnight after the examination on St Paul's theory of human nature, Mr and Mrs Cardew came as usual, and Catharine was one of the selected guests. The company sat round the table, and Mrs Cardew was placed between her husband and Miss Furze. The rector's wife was a fair-haired lady, with quiet, grey eyes, and regular, but not strikingly beautiful, features. Yet they were attractive, because they were harmonious, and betokened a certain inward agreement. It was a sane, sensible face, but a careless critic might have thought that it betokened an incapability of emotion, especially as Mrs Cardew had a habit of sitting back in her chair, and generally let the conversation take its own course until it came very close to her. She had a sober mode of statement and criticism, which was never brilliant and never stupid. It ought to have been most serviceable to her husband, because it might have corrected the exaggeration into which his impulse, talent, and power of pictorial representation were so apt to fall. She had been brought up as an Evangelical, but she had passed through no religious experiences whatever, and religion, in the sense in which Evangelicalism in the Church of England of that day understood it, was quite unintelligible to her. Had she been born a few years later she would have taken to science, and would have done well at it, but at that time there was no outlet for any womanly faculty, much larger in quantity than we are apt to suppose, which has an appetite for exact facts.

Mr Cardew would have been called a prig by those who did not know him well. He had a trick of starting subjects suddenly, and he very often made his friends very uncomfortable by the precipitate introduction, without any warning, of remarks upon serious matters. Once even, shocking to say, he quite unexpectedly at a tea-party made an observation about God. Really, however, he was not a prig. He was very sincere. He lived in a world of his own, in which certain figures moved which were as familiar to him as common life and he consequently talked about them. He leaned in front of his wife and said to Catharine –

'Have you read much, Miss Furze?'

'No, very little.'

'Indeed! I should have thought you were a reader. What have you read lately? any stories?'

'Yes, I have read Rasselas.'

'Rasselas! Have you really? Now tell me what you think of it.'

'Oh! I cannot tell you all.'

'No, it is not fair to put the question in that way. It is necessary to have some training in order to give a proper account of the scope and purpose of a book. Can you select any one part which struck you, and tell me why it struck you?

'The part about the astronomer. I thought all that is said about the dreadful effects of uncontrolled imagination was so wonderful.'

'Don't you think those effects are exaggerated?'

She lost herself for a moment, as we have already seen she was in the habit of doing, or rather, she did not lose herself, but everything excepting herself, and she spoke as if nobody but herself were present.

'Not in the least exaggerated. What a horror to pass days in dreaming about one particular thing, and to have no power to wake!'

Her head had fallen a little forward; she suddenly straightened herself; the blood rose in her face, and she looked very confused.

'I should like to preach about Dr Johnson,' said Mr Cardew.

'Really, Mr Cardew,' interposed the elder Miss Ponsonby, 'Dr Johnson is scarcely a sacred subject.'

'I beg your pardon; I do not mean preaching on the Sabbath. I should like to lecture about him. It is a curious thing, Miss Ponsonby, that although Johnson was such a devout Christian, yet in his troubles his remedy is generally nothing but that of the Stoics – courage and patience.'

Nobody answered, and an awkward pause followed. Catharine had not recovered from the shock of self-revelation, and the Misses Ponsonby were uneasy, not only because the conversation had taken such an unusual turn, but because a pupil had contributed. Mrs Cardew, distressed at her husband's embarrassment, ventured to come to the rescue.

'I think Dr Johnson quite right; when I am in pain, and nothing does me any good, I never have anything to say to myself, excepting that I must just be quiet, wait and bear it.'

This very plain piece of pagan common sense made matters worse. Mr Cardew seemed vexed that his wife had spoken, and there was once more silence for quite half a minute. Miss Adela Ponsonby then rang the bell, and Catharine in accordance with rule, left the room.

'Rather a remarkable young woman,' carelessly observed the rector.

'Decidedly!' said both the Misses Ponsonby, in perfect unison.

'She has been much neglected,' continued Miss Ponsonby. 'Her manners leave much to be desired. She has evidently not been accustomed to the forms of good society, or to express herself in accordance with the usual practice. We have endeavoured to impress upon her that, not only is much care necessary in the choice of topics of conversation, but in the mode of dealing with them. I thought it better not to encourage any further remarks from her, or I should have pointed out that, if what you say of Dr Johnson is correct, as I have no doubt it is, considering the party in the church to which he belonged, it only shows that he was unacquainted experimentally with the consolations of religion.'

'Isn't Mr Cardew a dear?' asked Miss Arden, when she and Catharine were together.

'I hardly understand what you mean, and I have not known Mr Cardew long enough to give any opinion upon him.'

'How exasperating you are again! You *do* know what I mean; but you always pretend never to know what anybody means.'

'I do *not* know what you mean.'

'Why isn't he handsome; couldn't you doat on him, and fall in love with him?'

'But he's married.'

'You fearful Catharine! of course he's married; you do take things so seriously.

'Well, I'm more in the dark than ever.'

'There you shall stick,' replied Miss Arden, lightly shaking her curls and laughing. 'Married! – yes, but they don't care for one another a straw.'

'Have they ever told you so?'

'How very ridiculous! Cannot you see for yourself?'

'I am not sure: it is very difficult to know whether people really love one another, and often equally difficult to know if they dislike one another.'

'What a philosopher you are! I'll tell you one thing, though: I believe he has just a little liking for me. Not for his life dare he show it. Oh, my goodness, wouldn't that fat be in the fire! Wouldn't there be a flare-up! What would the Ponsonbys do? Polite letter to papa announcing that my education was complete! That's what they did when Julia Jackson got in a mess. They couldn't have a scandal: so her education was complete, and home she went. Now the first time we are out for a walk and he passes us and bows, you watch.'

Miss Julia Arden went to sleep directly she went to bed, but Catharine, contrary to her usual customs, lay awake till she heard twelve o'clock strike from St Mary, Abchurch. She started, and thought that she alone, perhaps, of all the people who lay within reach of those chimes had heard them. Why did she not go to sleep? She was unused to wakefulness, and its novelty surprised her with all sorts of vague terrors. She turned from side to side anxiously while midnight sounded, but she was young, and in ten minutes afterwards she was dreaming. She was mistaken in supposing that she was the only person awake in Abchurch that night. Mrs Cardew heard the chimes, and over her their soothing melody had no power. When she and her husband left the Limes he broke out at once, with all the eagerness with which a man begins when he has been repeating to himself for some time every word of his grievance –

'I don't know how it is, Jane, but whenever I say anything I feel you are just the one person on whom it seems to make no impression. You have a trick of repetition, and you manage to

61

turn everything into a platitude. If you cannot do better than that, you might be silent.'

He was right so far, that it is possible by just a touch to convert the noblest sentiment into commonplace. No more than a touch is necessary. The parabolic mirror will reflect the star to a perfect focus. The elliptical mirror, varying from the parabola by less than the breadth of a hair, throws an image which is useless. But Mr Cardew was far more wrong than he was right. He did not take into account that what his wife said and what she felt might not be the same; that persons, who have no great command over language, are obliged to make one word do duty for a dozen, and that, if his wife was defective at one point, there were in her whole regions of unexplored excellence, of faculties never encouraged, and an affection to which he offered no response. He had not learned the art of being happy with her: he did not know that happiness is an art: he rather did everything he could do to make the relationship intolerable. He demanded payment in coin stamped from his own mint, and if bullion and jewels had been poured before him he would have taken no heed of them.

She said nothing. She never answered him when he was angry with her. It was growing dark as they went home, and the tears came into her eyes and the ball rose in her throat, and her lips quivered. She went back – does a woman ever forget them? – to the hours of passionate protestation before marriage, to the walks together when he caught up her poor phrases and refined them, and helped her to see herself, and tried also to learn what few things she had to teach. It was all the worse because she still loved him so dearly, and felt that behind the veil was the same face, but she could not tear the veil away. Perhaps, as they grew older, matters might become worse, and they might have to travel together estranged down the long, weary path to death. Death! She did not desire to leave him, but she would have lain down in peace to die that moment if he could be made to see her afterwards as she knew she was – at least in her love for him. But then she thought what suffering the remembrance of herself would cost him, and she wished to live. He felt that she moved her hand to her pocket, and he knew why it went there. He pitied her, but he pitied himself more, and though her tears wrought on him sufficiently to prevent any further cruelty, he did not repent.

CHAPTER VIII

Mrs Cardew met Catharine two or three times accidentally within the next fortnight. There were Dorcas meetings and meetings of all kinds at which the young women at the Limes were expected to assist. One afternoon, after tea, the room being hot, two or three of the company had gone out into the garden to work. Catharine and Mrs Cardew sat by themselves at one corner, where the ground rose a little, and a seat had been placed under a large ash tree. From that point St Mary's spire was visible, about half a mile away in the west, rising boldly, confidently, one might say, into the sky, as if it dared to claim that it too, although on earth and finite, could match itself against the infinite heaven above. On this particular evening the spire was specially obvious and attractive, for it divided the sunset clouds, standing out black against the long, narrow interspaces of tender green which lay between. It was one of those evenings which invite confidence, when people cannot help drawing nearer than usual to one another.

'Is it not beautiful, Miss Furze?'

'Beautiful; the spire makes it so lovely.'

'I wonder why.'

'I am sure I do not know; but it is so.'

'Catharine – you will not mind my calling you by your Christian name – you can explain it if you like.'

Catharine smiled. 'It is very kind of you, Mrs Cardew, to call me Catharine, but I have no explanation. I could not give one to save my life, unless it is the contrast.'

'You cannot think how I wish I had the power of saying what I think and feel. I cannot express myself properly – so my husband says.'

'I sympathise with you. I am so foolish at times. Mr Cardew, I should think, never felt the difficulty.'

'No, and he makes so much of it. He says I do not properly enjoy a thing if I cannot in some measure describe my enjoyment – articulate it, to use his own words.'

He had inwardly taunted her, even when she was suffering, and had said to himself that her trouble must be insignificant, for there was no colour nor vivacity in her description of it. She did not properly even understand his own shortcomings. He could pardon her criticism, so he imagined, if she could be pungent. Mistaken mortal! It was her patient heroism which made her dumb to him about her sorrows and his faults. A very limited vocabulary is all that is necessary on such topics.

'I am just the same.'

'Oh, no, you are not; Mr Cardew says you are not.'

'Mr Cardew? – he has not noticed anything in me, I am certain, and if he has, why nobody could be less able to talk to him than I am.'

Catharine knew nothing of what had passed between husband and wife – one scene amongst many – and consequently could not understand the peculiar earnestness, somewhat unusual with her, with which Mrs Cardew dwelt upon this subject. We lead our lives apart in close company with private hopes and fears unknown to anybody but ourselves, and when we go abroad we often appear inexplicable and absurd, simply because our friends have not the proper key.

'Do you think, Catharine – you know that, though I am older than you and married, I feel we are friends.' Here Mrs Cardew took Catharine's hand in hers. 'Do you think I could learn how to talk? What I mean is, could I be taught how to say what is appropriate? I *do* feel something when Mr Cardew reads Milton to me. It is only the words I want – words such as you have.'

'Oh, Mrs Cardew!' – Catharine came closer to her, and Mrs Cardew's arm crept round her waist – 'I tell you again I have not so many words as you suppose. I believe, though, that if people take pains they can find them.'

'Couldn't you help me?'

'I? Oh, no! Mr Cardew could. I never heard anybody express himself as he does.'

'Mr Cardew is a minister, and perhaps I should find it easier with you. Suppose I bring the "Paradise Lost" out into the garden when we next meet, and I will read, and you shall help me to comment on it.'

Catharine's heart went out towards her, and it was agreed that 'Paradise Lost' should be brought, and that Mrs Cardew would endeavour to make herself 'articulate' thereon. The party broke up, and Catharine's reflections were not of the simplest order. Rather let us say her emotions, for her heart was busier than her head. Mrs Cardew had deeply touched her. She never could stand unmoved the eyes of her dog when the poor beast came and laid her nose on her lap and looked up at her, and nobody could have persuaded her of the truth of Mr Cardew's doctrine that the reason why a dog can only bark is that his thoughts are nothing but barks. Mrs Cardew's appeal, therefore, was of a kind to stir her sympathy; but – had she not heard that Mr Cardew had observed and praised her? It was nothing – ridiculously nothing; it was his duty to praise and blame the pupils at the Limes; he had complimented Miss Toogood on her Bible history the other day, and on her satisfactory account of the scheme of Redemption. He had done it publicly, and he had pointed out the failings of the other pupils, she, Catharine, herself being included. He had reminded her that she had not taken into account the one vital point, that, as we are the Almighty Maker's creatures, His absolutely, we have no ground of complaint against Him in whatever way He may be pleased to make us. Nevertheless, just those two or three words Mrs Cardew reported were like yeast, and her whole brain was in a ferment.

The Milton was produced next week. Since Catharine had been at the Limes she had read some of it, incited by Mr Cardew, for he was an enthusiast for Milton. Mrs Cardew was a bad reader; she had no emphasis, no light and shade, and she missed altogether the rhythm of the verse. To Catharine, on the other hand, knowing nothing of metre, the proper cadence came easily. They finished the first six hundred lines of the first book.

'You have not said anything, Catharine.'

'No; but what have you to say?'

'It is very fine; but there I stick; I cannot say any more; I want

66

to say more; that is where I always am. I can *not* understand why I cannot go on as some people do; I just stop there with "very fine." '

'Cannot you pick out some passage which particularly struck you?'

'That is very true, is it not, that the mind can make a heaven of hell and a hell of heaven?'

'Most true; but did you not notice the description of the music?'

Catharine was fond of music, but only as an expression of her own feelings. For music as music – for a melody of Mozart, for example – that is to say, for pure art which is simply beauty, superior to our personality, she did not care. She liked Handel, and there was a choral society in Eastthorpe which occasionally performed the 'Messiah.'

'Don't you remember what Mr Cardew said about it – it was remarkable that Milton should have given to music the power to chase doubt from the mind, doubt generally, and yet music is not argument?'

'Oh, yes, I recollect, but I do not quite comprehend him, and I told him I did not see how music could make me sure of a thing if there was not a reason for it.'

'What did he say then?'

'Nothing.'

Mr Cardew called that evening to take his wife home. He was told that she was in the garden with Miss Furze, and thither he at once went.

'Milton!' he exclaimed. 'What are you doing with Milton here?'

'Miss Furze and I were reading the first book of the "Paradise Lost" together.'

Mrs Cardew looked at her husband inquiringly, and with a timid smile, hoping he would show himself pleased. His brow, however, slightly wrinkled itself with displeasure. He had told her to read Milton, had said, 'Fancy an Englishwoman with any pretensions to education not knowing Milton!' and now, when she was doing exactly what she was directed to do, he was vexed. He was annoyed to find he was precisely obeyed, and perhaps would have been in a better temper if he had been contradicted and resisted. Mrs Cardew turned her head away. What was she to do with him? Every one of her efforts to find the door had failed.

'What has struck you particularly in that book, Miss Furze?'

Catharine was about to say something, but she caught sight of Mrs Cardew, and was arrested. At last she spoke, but what she said was not what she at first had intended to say.

'Mrs Cardew and I were discussing the lines about doubt and music, and we cannot see what Milton means. We cannot see how music can make us sure of a thing if there is not good reason for it.'

Catharine used the first person plural with the best intention, but her object was defeated. The rector recognised the words at once.

'Yes, yes,' he replied, impatiently; 'but, Miss Furze, you know better than that. Milton does not mean doubt whether an arithmetical proposition is true. I question if he means theological doubt. Doubt in that passage is nearer despondency. It is despondency taking an intellectual form and clothing itself with doubts which no reasoning will overcome, which re-shape themselves the moment they are refuted.' He stopped for a moment. 'Don't you think so, Miss Furze?'

She forgot Mrs Cardew, and looked straight into Mr Cardew's face bent earnestly upon her.

'I understand.'

Mrs Cardew had lifted her eyes from the ground on which they had been fixed. 'I think,' said she, 'we had better be going.'

'We can go out by the door at the end of the garden, if you will go and bid the Misses Ponsonby good-bye.'

Mrs Cardew lingered a moment.

'I have bidden them good-bye,' said her husband.

She went, and Miss Ponsonby detained her for a few minutes to arrange the details of an important quarterly meeting of the Dorcas Society for next week.

'What do you think of the subject of the "Paradise Lost," Miss Furze?'

'I hardly know; it seems so far away.'

68

'Ah! that is just the point. I thought so once, but not now. Milton could not content himself with a common theme; nothing less than God and the immortal feud between Him and Satan would suffice. Milton is representative to me of what I may call the heroic attitude towards existence. Mark, too, the importance of man in the book. Men and women are not mere bubbles – here for a moment and then gone – but they are actually important, all-important, I may even say, to the Maker of the universe and His great enemy. In this Milton follows Christianity, but what stress he lays on the point! Our temptation, notwithstanding our religion, so often is to doubt our own value. All appearances tend to make us doubt it. Don't you think so?'

Catharine looked earnestly at the excited preacher, but said nothing.

'I do not mean our own personal worth. The temptation is to doubt whether it is of the smallest consequence whether we are or are not, and whether our being here is not an accident. Oh, Miss Furze, to think that your existence and mine are part of the Divine eternal plan, and that without us it would be wrecked! Then there is Satan. Milton has gone beyond the Bible, beyond what is authorised in giving such a distinct, powerful, and prominent individuality to Satan. You will remember that in the great celestial battle –

> ' "Long time in even scale
> The battle hung."

But what a wonderful conception that is of the great antagonist of God! It comes out even more strongly in the "Paradise Regained." Is it not a relief to think that the evil thought in you or me is not altogether yours and mine, but is foreign; that it is an incident in the war of wars, an attack on one of the soldiers of the Most High?'

Mr Cardew paused.

'Have you never written anything which I could read?'

'Scarcely anything. I wrote some time ago a little story of a few pages, but it was never published. I will lend you the manuscript, but you will please remember that it is anonymous, and that I do not wish the authorship revealed. I believe most people would not think any the better of me, certainly as a clergyman, if they knew it was mine.'

'That is very kind of you.'

Catharine felt the distinction, the confidence. The sweetest homage which can be offered us is to be entrusted with something which others would misinterpret.

'I should like, Miss Furze, to have some further talk to you about Milton, but I do not quite see' (musingly) 'how it is to be managed.'

'Could you not tell us something about him when you and Mrs Cardew next have tea with us at the Limes?'

'I do not think so. I meant with you, yourself. It is not easy for me to express myself clearly in company – at any rate, I should not hear your difficulties. You seem to possess a sympathy which is unusual, and I should be glad to know more of your mind.'

'When Mrs Cardew comes here, could you not fetch her, and could we not sit out here together?'

He hesitated. They were walking slowly over the grass towards the gate, and were just beginning to turn off to the right by the side path between the laurels. At that point, the lawn being levelled and raised, there were two steps. In descending them Catharine slipped, and he caught her arm. She did not fall, but he did not altogether release her for at least some seconds.

'Mrs Cardew has no liking for poetry.'

Catharine was silent.

'It is quite a new thing to me, Miss Furze, to find anybody in Abchurch who cares anything for that which is most interesting to me.'

'But, Mr Cardew, I am sure I have not shown any particular capacity, and I am very ignorant, for I have read very little.'

'It does not need much to reveal what is in a person. It would be a great help to me if we could read a book together. This self-imprisonment day after day and self-imposed reticence is very unwholesome. I would give much to have a pupil or a friend whose world is my world.'

To Catharine it seemed as if she was being sucked in by a

whirlpool and carried she knew not whither. They had reached the gate, and he had taken her hand in his to bid her good-bye. She felt a distinct and convulsive increase of pressure, and she felt also that she returned it. Suddenly something passed through her brain swift as the flash of the swiftest blazing meteor: she dropped his hand, and, turning instantly, went back to the house, retreating behind the thick bank of evergreens.

'Where is Miss Furze?' said Mrs Cardew, who came down the path a minute or two afterwards.

'I do not know: I suppose she is indoors.'

'A canting, hypocritical parson, type not uncommon, described over and over again in novels, and thoroughly familiar to theatre-goers.' Such, no doubt, will be the summary verdict passed upon Mr Cardew. The truth is, however, that he did not cant, and was not a hypocrite. One or two observations here may perhaps be pertinent. The accusation of hypocrisy, if we mean lofty assertion, and occasional and even conspicuous moral failure, may be brought against some of the greatest figures in history. But because David sinned with Bathsheba, and even murdered her husband, we need not discredit the sincerity of the Psalms. The man was inconsistent, it is true, inconsistent exactly because there was so much in him that was great, for which let us be thankful. Let us take notice, too, of what lies side by side quietly in our own souls. God help us if all that is good in us is to be invalidated by the presence of the most contradictory evil.

Secondly, it is a fact that vitality means passion. It does not mean avarice or any of the poor, miserable vices. If David had been a wealthy and pious Jerusalem shopkeeper, who subscribed largely to missionary societies to the Philistines, but who paid the poor girls in his employ only two shekels a week, refusing them ass-hire when they had to take their work three parts of the way to Bethlehem, and turning them loose at a minute's warning, he certainly would not have been selected to be part author of the Bible, even supposing his courtship and married life to have been most exemplary and orthodox. We will, however, postpone any further remarks upon Mr Cardew:

a little later we shall hear something about his early history, which may perhaps explain and partly exculpate him. As to Catharine, she escaped. It is vexatious that a complicated process in her should be represented by a single act which was transacted in a second. It would have been much more intelligible if it could have written itself in a dramatic conversation extending over two or three pages, but, as the event happened, so it must be recorded. The antagonistic and fiercely combatant forces did *so* issue in that deed, and the present historian has no intention to attempt an analysis. One thing is clear to him, that the quick stride up the garden path was urged not by any single, easily predominating impulse which had been enabled to annihilate all others. Do not those of us, who have been mercifully prevented from damning ourselves before the whole world, who have succeeded and triumphed – do we not know, know as we know hardly anything else, that our success and our triumph were due to superiority in strength by just a grain, no more, of our better self over the raging rebellion beneath it? It was just a tremble of the tongue of the balance: it might have gone this way, or it might have gone the other, but by God's grace it was this way settled – God's grace, as surely, in some form of words, everybody must acknowledge it to have been. When she reached her bedroom she sat down with her head on her hands, rose, walked about, looked out of window in the hope that she might see him, thought of Mrs Cardew; forgot her; dwelt on what she had passed through till she almost actually felt the pressure of his hand; cursed herself that she had turned away from him; prayed for strength to resist temptation, and longed for one more chance of yielding to it.

The next morning a little parcel was left for Miss Furze. It contained the promised story, which is here presented to my readers:–

"Did he Believe?

'Charmides was born in Greece, but about the year 300 A.D. was living in Rome. He had come there, like many of his countrymen, to pursue his calling as sculptor in the imperial city, and he cherished a great love for his art. He knew too well that it was not the art of the earlier days of Athens, and that he could never catch the spirit of that golden time, but he loved it none the less. He was also a philosopher in his way. He had read not only the literature of Greece, but that of his adopted land, and he was especially familiar with Lucretius and his pupil Virgil. His intellectual existence, however, was not particularly happy. Rome was a pleasant city; his occupation was one in which he delighted; the thrill of a newly noticed Lucretian idea or of a tender touch in Virgil were better to him than any sensual pleasure, but his dealings with his favourite authors ended in his own personal emotion, and it was sad to think that the Hermes on which he had spent himself to such a degree should become a mere decoration to a Roman nobleman's villa, valued only because it cost so much, and that nobody who looked at it would ever really care for it. Once, however, he was rewarded. He had finished a Pallas Athene just as the sun went down. He was excited, and after a light sleep he rose very early and went into the studio with the dawn. There stood the statue, severe, grand in the morning twilight, and if there was one thing in the world clear to him, it was that what he saw was no inanimate mineral mass, but something more. It was no mere mineral mass with an outline added. Part of the mind which formed the world was in it, actually in it, and it came to Charmides that intellect, thought, had their own rights, that they were as much a fact as the stone, and that what he had done was simply to realise a Divine idea which was immortal, no matter what might become of its embodiment. The weight of the material world lifted, an avenue of escape seemed to open itself to him from so much that oppressed and deadened him, and he felt like a man in an amphitheatre of overhanging mountains, who should espy in a far-off corner some scarcely perceptible track, and on nearer inspection a break in the walled precipices, a promise or at least a hint, of a passage from imprisonment to the open plain. It was nothing more than he had learned in his Plato, but the truth was made real to him, and he clung to it.

'Rome at the end of the third century was one of the most licentious of cities. It was invaded by all the vices of Greece, and

73

the counterpoise of the Greek virtues was absent. The reasoning powers assisted rather than prevented the degradation of morals, for they dissected and represented as nothing all the motives which had hitherto kept men upright. The healthy and uncorrupted instinct left to itself would have been a sufficient restraint, but sophistry argued and said, *What is there in it?* – and so the very strength and prerogative of man hired itself out to perform the office of making him worse than a beast. Charmides was unmarried, and it is not to be denied that though his life as a whole was pure, he had yielded to temptation, not without loathing himself afterwards. He did not feel conscious of any transgression of a moral law, for no such law was recognised, but he detested himself because he had been drawn into close contact with a miserable wretch simply in order to satisfy a passion, and in the touch of mercenary obscenity there was something horrible to him. It was bitter to him to reflect that, notwithstanding his aversion from it, notwithstanding his philosophy and art, he had been equally powerless with the uttermost fool of a young aristocrat to resist the attraction of the commonest of snares. What were his books and fine pretensions worth if they could not protect him in such ordinary danger? Thus it came to pass that after a fall, when he went back to his work, it was so unreal to him, such a mockery, that days often elapsed before he could do anything. It was a mere toy, a dilettante dissipation, the embroidery of corruption. Oh, for a lawgiver, for a time of restraint, for the time of Regulus and the republic! Then, said Charmides to himself, my work would have some value, for heroic obedience would be behind it. He was right, for the love of the beautiful cannot long exist where there is moral pollution. The love of the beautiful itself is moral – that is to say, what we love in it is virtue. A perfect form or a delicate colour are the expression of something which is destroyed in us by subjugation to the baser desires or meanness, and he who has been unjust to man or woman misses the true interpretation of a cloud or falling wave.

'One night Charmides was walking through the lowest part of the city, and he heard from a mere hovel the sound of a hymn. He knew what it was – that it was the secret celebration of a religious rite by the despised sect of the Jews and their wretched proselytes. The Jews were especially hateful to him and to all cultured people in Rome. They were typical of all the qualities which culture abhorred. No Jew had ever produced anything lovely in any department whatever – no picture, statue, melody, nor poem. Their literature was also barbaric: there was no consecutiveness in it, no reasoning, no recognition in fact of the reason. It was a mere mass of legends without the exquisite charm and spiritual intention of those of Greece, of bloody stories and obscure disconnected prophecies by shepherds and peasants. Their god was a horror, a boor upon a mountain, wielding thunder and lightning. Aphrodite was perhaps not all that could be wished, but she was divine compared with the savage Jehovah. It was true that a recent Jewish sect professed better things and recognised as their teacher a young malefactor who was executed when Tiberius was emperor. So far, however, as could be made out he was a poor crack-brained demagogue, who dreamed of restoring a native kingdom in Palestine. What made the Jews especially contemptible to culture was that they were retrograde. They strove to put back the clock. There is only one path, so culture affirmed, and that is the path opened by Aristotle, the path of rational logical progress from what we already know to something not now known, but which can be known. If our present state is imperfect, it is because we do not know enough. Every other road, excepting this, the king's highway, leads into a bog. These Jews actually believed in miracles; they had no science, and thought they could regenerate the world by hocus-pocus. They ought to be suppressed by law, and, if necessary, put to death for they bred discontent.

'Nevertheless, Charmides decided to enter the hovel. He was in an idle mood, and he was curious to see for himself what the Jews were like. He pushed open the door, and when he went in he found himself in a low mean room very dimly lighted and crowded with an odd medley of Greeks, Romans, tolerably well-dressed persons, and slaves. The poor and the slaves were by far the most numerous. The atmosphere was stifling, and Charmides sat as near the door as possible. Next to him was a slave-girl, not beautiful, but with a peculiar expression on her face very rare in Rome at that time. The Roman women were, many of them, lovely, but their loveliness was cold – the loveliness of indifference. The somewhat common features of this slave, on the contrary, were lighted up with eagerness: to her there was evidently something in life of consequence – nay, of immense importance. There were few of her betters in Rome to whom anything was of importance. A hymn at that moment was being sung, the words of which Charmides could not catch, and when it was finished an elderly man rose and read what seemed the strangest jargon about justification and sin. The very terms used were in fact unintelligible. The extracts were from a letter addressed to the sect in Rome by one Paul, a disciple of that Jesus who was crucified. After the reading was over came an address, very wild in tone and gesture, and equally unintelligible, and then a prayer or invocation, partly to their god, but also, as it seemed, to this Jesus, who evidently ranked as a dæmon, or perhaps as Divine. Charmides was quite unaffected. The whole thing appeared perfect nonsense, not worth investigation, but he could not help wondering what there was in it which could so excite that girl, whom he could hardly conclude to be a fool, and whose earnestness was a surprise to him. He thought no more about the affair until some days afterwards when he happened to visit a friend. Just as he was departing he met this very slave in the porch. He involuntarily stopped, and she whispered to him.

' "You will not betray us?"

' "I! Certainly not."

' "I will lend you this. Read it and return it to me." So saying, she vanished.

'Charmides, when he reached home, took out the manuscript. He recognised it as a copy of the letter which he had partly heard at the meeting. He was somewhat astonished to find that it was written by a man of learning, who was evidently familiar with classic authors, but surely never was scholarship pressed into such a service! The confusion of metaphor, the suddenness of transition, the illogical muddles were bad enough, but the chief obstacle to comprehension was that the author's whole scope

76

and purpose, the whole circle of his ideas, were outside Charmides altogether. He was not attracted any more than he was at the meeting, but he was a little piqued because Paul had certainly been well educated, and he determined to attend the meeting again. This time he was late, and did not arrive till it was nearly at an end. His friend was there, and again he sat down next to her. When they went out it was dark, and he walked by her side.

' "Have you read the letter?"

' "Yes, but I do not understand it, and I have brought it back."

' "May Christ the Lord open your eyes!"

' "Who is this Christ whom you worship?"

' "The Son of God, He who was crucified; the man Jesus; He who took upon Himself flesh to redeem us from our sins; in whom by faith we are justified and have eternal life."

'It was all pure Hebrew to him, save the phrase "Son of God," which sounded intelligible.

' "You are Greek," he said, for he recognised her accent although she spoke Latin.

' "Yes, from Corinth: my name is Demariste"; and she explained to him that, although she was a slave, she was partly employed in teaching Greek to the children of her mistress.

' "If you are Greek and well brought up, you must know that I cannot comprehend a word of what you have spoken. It is Judaism."

' "To me, too," she replied, speaking Greek to him, "it was incomprehensible, but God by the light which lighteth every man hath brought me into His marvellous light, and now this that I have told you is exceedingly clear – nay, clearer than anything which men say they see."

' "Tell me how it happened."

' "When I first came to Rome I had a master who desired to make me his concubine, and I hated him; but what strength had I? – and I was tempted to yield. My parents were dead; I had no friends who cared for me – what did it matter! I had read in my books of the dignity of the soul, but that was a poor weapon with which to fight, and moreover sin was not exceeding sinful to me.

77

By God's grace I was brought amongst these Christians, and I was convinced of sin. I saw that it was not only transgression against myself, but against the eternal decrees of the Most High, against those decrees which, as one of our own poets still dear to me has said –

' " Ού γάρ τι νῦν γε κἀχθὲς, ἀλλ' ἀεί ποτε
ζῆ ταῦτα, κοὐδεὶς οἰδεν ἐξ ὅτου 'φάνη."[1]

' "I saw that all art, all learning, everything which men value, were as straw compared with God's commands, and that it would be well to destroy all our temples, and statues, and all that we have which is beautiful, if we could thereby establish the kingdom of God within us, and so become heirs of the life everlasting. Oh, my friend, my friend in Christ, I hope, believe me, Rome will perish, and we shall all perish, not because we are ignorant, but because we have not obeyed His word. But how was I to obey it? Then I heard told the life of Christ the Lord: how God the Father in His infinite pity sent His Son into the world; how He lived amongst us and died a shameful death upon the cross that we might not die; and all His strength passed into me and became mine through faith, and I was saved; saved for this life; saved eternally; justified through Him; worthy to wait for Him and meet Him at His coming, for He shall come, and I shall be for ever with the Lord."

'Demariste stood straight upright as she spoke, and the light in her transfigured her countenance as the sun penetrating a grey mass of vapour informs it with such an intensity of brightness that the eye can scarcely endure it. It was a totally new experience to Charmides, an entire novelty in Rome. He did not venture to look in her face directly, for he felt that there was nothing in him equal to its sublime, solemn pleading.

' "I do not know anything of your Jesus," he said at last, timidly; "upon what do you rest His claims?"

' "Read His life. I will lend it to you; you will want no other evidence for Him. And was He not raised from the dead to reign

'Not now nor of yesterday are they, but for ever they live, and no one knows whence to date their appearance.' – *Sophocles*, *'Antigone.'*

78

for ever at His Father's right hand? No, keep the letter for a little while, and perhaps you will understand it better when you know upon what it is based."

'A day or two afterwards the manuscript was sent to him secretly with many precautions. He was not smitten suddenly by it. The Palestinian tale, although he confessed it was much more to his mind than Paul, was still *rude*. It was once more the rudeness which was repellent, and which almost outweighed the pathos of many of the episodes and the undeniable grandeur of the trial and death. Moreover, it was full of superstition and supernaturalism, which he could not abide. He was in his studio after its first perusal, and he turned to an Apollo which he was carving. The god looked at him with such overpowering, balanced sanity, such a contrast to Christian incoherence and the rhapsodies of the letter to the Romans, that he was half ashamed of himself for meddling with it. He opened his Lucretius. Here was order and sequence; he knew where he was; he was at home. Was all this nought, were the accumulated labour and thought of centuries to be set aside and trampled on by the crude, frantic inspiration of clowns? The girl's face, however, recurred to him; he could not get rid of it, and he opened the biography again. He stumbled upon what now stand as our twenty-third and twenty-fourth chapters of Matthew, containing the denunciation of the Pharisees, and the prophecy of the coming of the Son of Man. He was amazed at the new turn which was given to life, at the reasons assigned for the curses which were dealt to these Jewish doctors. They were damned for their lack of mercy, judgment, faith, for their extortion, excess, and because they were full of hypocrisy and iniquity. They were fools and blind, but not through defects which would have condemned them in Greece and Rome at that day, but through failings of which Greece and Rome took small account. Charmides pondered and pondered, and saw that this Jew had given a new centre, a new pivot to society. This, then, was the meaning of the world as nearly as it could be said to have a single meaning. Read by the light of the twenty-third chapter, the twenty-fourth chapter was magnificent. "For as the lightning cometh out of the east, and shineth even unto the west, so shall the coming of the Son of Man be." Was it not intelligible that He to whom right and wrong were so diverse, to whom their diversity was the one fact for man, should believe that Heaven would proclaim and enforce it? He read more and more, until at last the key was given to him to unlock even that strange mystery, that being justified by faith we have peace with God through our Lord Jesus Christ. Still it was idle for him to suppose that he could ever call himself a Christian in the sense in which those poor creatures whom he had seen were Christians. Their fantastic delusions, their expectation that any day the sky might open and their Saviour appear in the body, were impossible to him; nor could he share their confidence that once for all their religion alone was capable of regenerating the world. He could not, it is true, avoid the reflection that the point was not whether the Christians were absurd, nor was it even the point whether Christianity was not partly absurd. The real point was whether there was not more certainty in it than was to be found in anything at that time current in the world. Here, in what Paul called faith, was a new spring of action, a new reason for the blessed life, and, what was of more consequence, a new force by which men might be enabled to persist in it. He could not, we say, avoid this reflection; he could not help feeling that he was bound not to wait for that which was in complete conformity with an ideal, but to enlist under the flag which was carried by those who in the main fought for the right, and that it was treason to cavil and stand aloof because the great issue was not presented in perfect purity. Nevertheless, he was not decided, and could not quite decide. If he could have connected Christianity with his own philosophy; if it had been the outcome, the fulfilment of Plato, his duty would have been so much simpler; it was the complete rupture – so it seemed to him – which was the difficulty. His heart at times leaped up to join this band of determined, unhesitating soldiers; to be one in an army; to have a cause; to have a banner waving over his head; to have done with isolation, aloofness, speculation ending in nothing, and dreams which profited nobody; but even in those moments when he was nearest to a confession of discipleship he was restrained by faintness and doubt. If he were to enrol himself as a convert his conversion would be due not to an irresistible impulse, but to a theory, to a calculation, one might almost say, that such and such was the proper course to take.

'He went again to the meeting, and he went again and again. One night, as he came home, he walked as he had walked before, with Demariste. She was going as far as his door for the manuscript which he had now copied for his own use. As they went along a man met them who raised a lantern, and directed it full in their faces.

' "The light of death," said Demariste.

' "Who is he?"

' "I know him well; he is a spy. I have often seen him at the door of our assembly."

' "Do you fear death?"

' "I? Has not Christ died?"

'Charmides had fallen in love with this slave, but it was love so different from any love which he had felt before for a woman, that it ought to have had some other name. It was a love of the soul, of that which was immortal, of God in her; it was a love, too, of no mere temporary phenomenon, but of reality outlasting death into eternity. There was thus a significance, there was a grandeur in it wanting to any earthly love. It was the new love with which men were henceforth to love women – the love of Dante for Beatrice.

'She waited at the door while he went inside to fetch the parchment. He brought it out and gave it to her, and as he stood opposite to her he looked in her face, and her eyes were not averted. He caught her hand, but she drew back.

' " 'Tis but for a day or two," she said; "a week will see the end."

' "A week!" he cried. "Oh, my Demariste, rather a week with thee than an age with anything less than thee!"

' "You will have to die too. Dare you die? The spirit may be willing, but the flesh may be weak."

' "Death! Yes, death, if only I am yours!"

' "Nay, nay, my beloved, not for me, but for the Lord Jesus."

'He bent nearer to her; his head was on her neck, and his arms were round her body. Oh, son and daughter of Time! oh, son and daughter of Eternity!

'He had hardly returned to his house, when he was interrupted by his friend Callippus, just a little the worse for wine.

' "What new thing is this?" said Callippus. "I hear you have consorted with the Jews, and have been seen at their assembly."

' "True, my friend."

' "True! By Jupiter! what is the meaning of it? You do not mean to say that you are bitten by the mad dog?"

' "I believe."

' "Oh, by God, that it should have come to this! Are you not ashamed to look him in the face?" pointing to the Apollo statue. "Ah! the old prophecy is once more verified! –

' "Tutemet a nobis iam quovis tempore vatum
terriloquis victus dictis desciscere quæres."[1]

But I must be prudent. I saw somebody watching your house on the other side of the street. If I am caught they will think I belong to the accursed sect too. Farewell."

'The morning came, and about an hour after Charmides had risen two soldiers presented themselves. He was hurried away, brought before the judges, and examined. Some little pity was felt for him by two or three members of the court, as he was well known in Rome, and one of them condescended to argue with him and to ask him how he could become ensnared by a brutal superstition which affirmed, so it was said, the existence of devil-possessed pigs, and offered sacrifices to them.

' "You," said he, "an artist and philosopher – if it be true that you are a pervert, you deserve a heavier punishment than the scum whom we have hitherto convicted."

' "For Christ and His cross!" cried Charmides.

' "Take him away!"

'The next day Charmides and Demariste met outside the prison gates. They were chained together in mockery, the seducer, Demariste, and the seduced, Charmides. They were

'You, yourself, some time or other, overcome by the terror-speaking tales of the seers, will seek to fall away from us.' – *Lucretius*, '*De Rerum Natura*.'

marched through the streets of Rome, the crowd jeering them and thronging after them to enjoy the sport of their torments and death. Charmides saw the eyes of Demariste raised heavenwards and her lips moving in prayer.

' "He has heard me," she said, "and you will endure."

'He pressed her hand, and replied, with unshaken voice, "Fear not."

'They came to the place of execution, but before the final stroke they were cruelly tortured. Charmides bore his sufferings in silence, but in her extremest agony the face of Demariste was lighted with rapture.

' "Look, look, my beloved, there, there!" trying to lift her mangled arm, "Christ the Lord! One moment more and we are for ever with Him."

'Charmides could just raise his head, and saw nothing but Demariste. He was able to turn himself towards her and move her hand to his lips, the second, only the second and the last kiss.

'So they died. Charmides was never considered a martyr by the Church. The circumstances were doubtful, and it was not altogether clear that he deserved the celestial crown.'

CHAPTER IX

The school broke up next week for the summer holidays, and Catharine went home. Her mother was delighted with her daughter. She was less awkward, straighter, and her air and deportment showed the success of the plan. The father acquiesced, although he did not notice the change till Mrs Furze had pointed it out. As to Mrs Bellamy, she declared, when she met Catharine in the street the first market afternoon that 'she had all at once become a woman grown.' Mrs Furze's separation from her former friends was now complete, but she had, unfortunately, not yet achieved admission into the superior circle. She had done so in a measure, but she was not satisfied. She felt that these people were not intimate with her, and that, although she had screwed herself with infinite pains into a bowing acquaintance, and even into a shaking of hands, they formed a set by themselves, with their own secrets and their own mysteries, into which she could not penetrate. Their very politeness was more annoying than rudeness would have been. It showed they could afford to be polite. Had she been wealthy, she could have crushed all opposition by sheer weight of bullion; but in Eastthorpe everybody's position was known with tolerable exactitude, and nobody was deluded into exaggerating Mr Furze's resources because of the removal to the Terrace. Eastthorpe, on the contrary, affirmed that the business had not improved, and that expenses had increased.

When Catharine came home a light suddenly flashed across Mrs Furze's mind. What might not be done with such a girl as that! She was good-looking – nay, handsome; she had the manners which Mrs Furze knew that she herself lacked, and Charlie Colston, aged twenty-eight, was still disengaged. It was Mrs Furze's way, when she proposed anything to herself, to take no account of any obstacles, and she had the most wonderful knack of belittling and even transmuting all moral objections. Mr Charlie Colston was a well-known figure in Eastthorpe. He was an only son, about five feet eleven inches high, thin, unsteady on his legs, smooth-faced, unwholesome, and silly. He had been taken into his father's business because there was nothing else for him, and he was a mere shadow in it, despised by every cask-washer. There was nothing wicked recorded against him; he did not drink, he did not gamble, he cared nothing for horses or dogs; but Eastthorpe thought none the better of him for these negative virtues. He was not known to be immoral, but he was for ever playing with this girl or the other, smiling, mincing, toying, and it all came to nothing. A very unpleasant creature was Mr Charlie Colston, a byword with women in Eastthorpe, even amongst the nursery-maids. Mrs Furze knew all about this youth; but she brought out her philosopher's stone and used it with effect. She did not intend to mate Catharine with a fool, and make her miserable. If she could not have persuaded herself that the young man was everything that could be desired she would have thought no more about him. The whole alchemical operation, however, of changing him into purest gold occupied only a few minutes, and the one thought now was how to drop the bait. It did cross her mind that Catharine herself might object; but she was convinced that if her daughter could have a distinct offer made to her, all opposition might somehow be quenched.

Fate came to her assistance, as it does always to those who watch persistently and with patience. One Sunday evening at church it suddenly began to rain. The Furze family had not provided themselves with umbrellas, but Mrs Furze knew that Mr Charlie Colston never went out without one. Her strategy, when the service was over, was worthy of Napoleon, and, with all the genius of a great commander, she brought her forces into exact position at the proper moment. She herself and Mr Furze detained the elder Mr Colston and his wife, and kept them in check a little way behind, so that Catharine and their son were side by side when the entrance was reached. Of course he could do nothing but offer Catharine his umbrella, and his company on the way homewards, but to his utter amazement, and the confusion of Mrs Furze, who watched intently the result of her manoeuvres, Catharine somewhat curtly declined, and turned back to wait for her parents. Mr Charlie rejoined his father and mother, who naturally forsook the Furzes at the earliest possible moment in such a public place as a church porch. In a few minutes the shower abated. Mrs Furze could not say anything to her daughter; she could not decently appear to force Charlie on her by rebuking her for not responding to his generosity, but she was disappointed and embittered.

On the following morning Catharine announced her intention of going to Chapel Farm for a few days. Her mother remonstrated, but she knew she would have to yield, and Catharine went. Mrs Bellamy poured forth the pent-up tale of three months – gossip we may call it if we wish to be contemptuous; but what is gossip? A couple of neighbours stand at the garden gate on a summer's evening and tell the news of the parish. They discuss the inconsistency of the parson, the stony-heartedness of the farmer, the behaviour of this young woman and that young man; and what better could they do? They certainly deal with what they understand – something genuinely within their own circle and experience; and there is nothing to them in politics, British or Babylonian, of more importance. There is no better conversation than talk about Smith, Brown, and Harris, male and female, about Spot the terrier or Juno the mare. Catharine had many questions to answer about the school, but Mr Cardew's name was not once mentioned.

One afternoon, late in August, Catharine had gone with the dog down to the riverside, her favourite haunt. Clouds, massive, white, sharply outlined, betokening thunder, lay on the horizon in a long line; the fish were active; great chub rose, and every now and then a scurrying dimple on the pool showed that the jack and the perch were busy. It was a day full of heat, a day of exultation, for it proclaimed that the sun was alive; it was a day on which to forget winter with its doubts, its despairs, and its indistinguishable grey; it was a day on which to believe in immortality. Catharine was at that happy age when summer has power to warm the brain; it passed into her blood and created in her simple, uncontaminated bliss. She sat down close to an alder which overhung the bank. It was curious, but so it was, that her thoughts suddenly turned from the water and the thunder-clouds and the blazing heat to Mr Cardew, and it is still more strange that at that moment she saw him coming along the towing-path. In a minute he was at her side, but before he reached her she had risen.

'Good morning, Miss Furze.'

'Mr Cardew! What brings you here?'

'I have been here several times; I often go out for the day; it is a favourite walk.'

He was silent, and did not move. He seemed prepossessed and anxious, taking no note of the beauty of the scene around him.

'How is Mrs Cardew?'

'She is well, I believe.'

'You have not left home this morning, then?'

'No; I was not at home last night.'

'I think I must be going.'

'I will walk a little way with you.'

'My way is over the bridge to the farmhouse, where I am staying.'

'I will go as far as you go.'

Catharine turned towards the bridge.

'Is it the house beyond the meadows?'

'Yes.'

It is curious how indifferent conversation often is just at the moment when the two who are talking may be trembling with passion.

'You should have brought Mrs Cardew with you,' said Catharine, tearing to pieces a water lily, and letting the beautiful white petals fall bit by bit into the river.

Mr Cardew looked at her steadfastly, scrutinisingly, but her eyes were on the thunderclouds, and the lily fell faster and faster. The face of this girl had hovered before him for weeks, day and night. He never for a moment proposed to himself deliberate love for her – he could not do it, and yet he had come there, not, perhaps, consciously in order to find her, but dreaming of her all the time. He was literally possessed. The more he thought about her, the less did he see and hear of the world outside him, and no motive for action found access to him which was not derived from her. Of course it was all utterly mad and unreasonable, for, after all, what did he really know about her, and what was there in her to lay hold of him with such strength? But, alas! thus it was, thus he was made; so much the worse for him. Was this a Christian believer? was he really sincere in his belief? He was sincere with a sincerity, to speak arithmetically, of the tenth power beyond that of his exemplary churchwarden Johnson, whose religion would have restrained him from anything warmer than the extension of a Sunday black-gloved finger-tip to any woman save 'Mrs J.' Here he was by the riverside with her; he was close to her; nobody was present, but he could not stir nor speak! Catharine felt his gaze, although her eyes were not towards him. At last the lily came to an end, and she tossed the naked stalk after the flower. She loved this man; it was a perilous moment: one touch, a hair's breadth of oscillation, and the two would have been one. At such a crisis the least external disturbance is often decisive. The first note of the thunder was heard, and suddenly the image of Mrs Cardew presented itself before Catharine's eyes, appealing to her piteously, tragically. She faced Mr Cardew.

'I am sorry Mrs Cardew is not here. I wish I had seen more of her. Oh, Mr Cardew! how I envy her! how I wish I had her brains for scientific subjects! She is wonderful. But I *must* be going; the thunder is distant: you will be in Eastthorpe, I hope, before the storm comes. Good-bye,' and she had gone.

She did not go straight to the house, however, but went into the garden and again cursed herself that she had dismissed him. Who had dismissed him? Not she. How had it been done? She could not tell. She crept out of the garden and went to the corner of the meadow where she could see the bridge. He was still there. She tried to make up an excuse for returning; she tried to go back without one, but it was impossible. Something, whatever it was, stopped her; she struggled and wrestled, but it was of no avail, and she saw Mr Cardew slowly retrace his steps to the town. Then she leaned upon the wall and found some relief in a great fit of sobbing. Consolation she had none; not even the poor reward of conscience and duty. She had lost him, and she felt that, if she had been left to herself, she would have kept him. She went out again late in the evening. The clouds had passed away to the south and east, but the lightning still fired the distant horizon far beyond Eastthorpe and towards Abchurch. The sky was clearing in the west, and suddenly in a rift Arcturus, about to set, broke through and looked at her, and in a moment was again eclipsed. What strange confusion! What inexplicable contrasts! Terror and divinest beauty; the calm of the infinite interstellar space and her own anguish; each an undoubted fact, but each to be taken by itself as it stood: the star was there, the dark blue depth was there, but they were no answer to the storm or her sorrow.

She returned to Eastthorpe on the following day and immediately told her mother she should not go back to the Misses Ponsonby.

CHAPTER X

The reader has, doubtless, by this time judged with much severity not only Catharine, but Mr Cardew. It is admitted to the full that they are both most unsatisfactory and most improbable. Is it likely that in a sleepy Midland town, such as Eastthorpe, knowing nothing but the common respectabilities of the middle of this century, the daughter of an ironmonger would fall in love with a married clergyman? Perhaps to their present biographer it seems more remarkable than to his readers. He remembers what the Eastern Midlands were like fifty years ago and they do not. They are thinking of Eastthorpe of the present day, of its schoolgirls who are examined in Keats and Shelley, of the Sunday morning walks there, and of the, so to speak, smelling acquaintance with sceptical books and theories which half the population now boasts. But Eastthorpe, when Mr Cardew was at Abchurch, was totally different. It knew what it was for parsons to go wrong. It had not forgotten a former rector and the young woman at the Bell. What talk there was about that affair! Happily his friends were well connected: they exerted themselves, and he obtained a larger sphere of usefulness two hundred miles away. Mr Cardew, however, was not that rector, and Catharine was not the pretty waitress, and it is time now to tell the promised early history of Mr Cardew.

He was the son of a well-to-do London merchant, who lived in Stockwell, in a large, white house, with a garden of a couple of acres, shaded by a noble cedar in its midst. There were four children, but he was the only boy. His mother belonged to an old and very religious family, and inherited all its traditions of Calvinistic piety and decorum. Her love for this boy was boundless, and she had a double ambition for him, which was that he might become a minister of God's Word, and in due time might marry Jane Berdoe, the only daughter of the Reverend

Charles Berdoe, M.A., and Euphemia, her dearest friend. Mrs Cardew had heard so much of the contamination of boys' schools that Theophilus was educated at home and sent straight from home to Cambridge. At the University he became a member of the ultra-evangelical sect of young men there, and devoted himself entirely to theology. He thus passed through youth and early manhood without any intercourse with the world so called, and he lacked that wholesome influence which is exercised by healthy companionship with those who differ from us and are not afraid to oppose us. Of course he married Jane Berdoe. His mother was always contriving that Jane should be present when he was at home: he was young: he had never known what it was to go astray with women, and he was unable to stand at a distance from her and ask himself if he really cared for her. He fell in love with himself, married himself, and soon after discovered that he did not know who his wife was. After his marriage he became wholly unjust to her, and allowed her defects to veil the whole of her character.

The ultra-evangelical school in the Church preserved at that time the religious life of England, although in a very strange form. They believed and felt certain vital truths, although they did not know what was vital and what was not. They had real experience, and their roots lay, not upon the surface, but went deep down to the perennial springs, and the articles of their creed became a vehicle for the expression of the most real emotions. Evangelicalism, however, to Mr Cardew was dangerous. He was always prone to self-absorption, and the tendency was much increased by his religion. He lived an entirely interior life, and his joys and sorrows were not those of Abchurch, but of another sphere. Abchurch feared wet weather, drought, ague, rheumatism, loss of money, and, on Sundays, feared hell, but Mr Cardew's fears were spiritual or even spectral. His self-communion produced one strange and perilous result, a habit of prolonged evolution from particular ideas uncorrected by reference to what was around him. If anything struck him it remained with him, deduction followed deduction in practice unfortunately as well as in thought, and he was ultimately landed in absurdity or something worse. The wholesome influence of ordinary men and women never permits us to link conclusion to conclusion from a single premiss, or at any rate to act upon our conclusions, but Mr Cardew had no world at Abchurch save himself. He saw himself in things, and not as they were. A sunset was just what it might happen to symbolise to him at the time, and his judgments upon events and persons were striking, but they were frequently judgments upon creations of his own imagination, and were not in the least apposite to what was actually before him. The happy, artistic, Shakespearian temper, mirroring the world like a lake, was altogether foreign to him.

When he saw Catharine a new love awoke in him instantaneously. Was it legitimate or illegitimate? In many cases of the same kind the answer would be that the question is one which cannot be put. No matter how pure the intellectual bond between man and woman may be, it is certain to carry with it a sentiment which cannot be explained by the attraction of mere mental similarity. A man says to a man, 'Do you really believe it?' and, if the answer is 'yes', the two become friends; but if it is a woman who responds to him, something follows which is sweeter than friendship, whether she be bound or free. It cannot be helped; there is no reason why we should try to help it, provided only we do no harm to others, and indeed these delicate threads are the very fairest in the tissue of life. With Mr Cardew it was a little different. Undoubtedly he was drawn to Catharine because her thoughts were his thoughts. St Paul and Milton in him saluted St Paul and Milton in her. But he did not know where to stop, nor could he look round and realise whither he was being led. Any other person in six weeks would have noticed the milestones on the road, and would have determined that it was time to turn, but he gaily walked forward with his head in the clouds. If anybody at that particular moment when he left the bridge could have made him comprehend that he was making love to a girl; that what he was doing was an ordinary, common-place criminal act, or one which would justifiably be interpreted as such, he not only would have been staggered and confounded, but would instantly have drawn back. As it was, he was neither staggered nor confounded, and went home to his wife with but one image in his brain, that of Catharine Furze.

Catharine was one of those creatures whose life is not uniform from sixteen to sixty, a simple progressive accumulation of experiences, the addition of a ring of wood each year. There had come a time to her when she had suddenly opened. The sun shone with new light, a new lustre lay on river and meadow, the stars became something more than mere luminous points in the sky, she asked herself strange questions, and she loved more than ever her long wanderings at Chapel Farm. This phenomenon of a new birth is more often seen at some epochs than at others. When a nation is stirred by any religious movement it is common, but it is also common in a different shape during certain periods of spiritual activity, such as the latter part of the eighteenth century and the first half of the nineteenth in England and Germany. Had Catharine been born two hundred years earlier, life would have been easy. All that was in her would have found expression in the faith of her ancestors, large enough for any intellect or any heart at that time. She would have been happy in the possession of a key which unlocks the mystery of things, and there would have been ample room for emotion. How impatient she became of those bars which nowadays restrain people from coming close to one another! Often and often she felt that she could have leaped out towards the person talking to her, that she could have cried to him to put away his circumlocutions, his forms and his trivialities, and to let her see and feel what he really was. Often she knew what it was to thirst like one in a desert for human intercourse, and she marvelled how those who pretended to care for her could stay away so long: she could have humiliated herself if only they would have permitted her to love them and be near them. Poor Catharine! the world as it is now is no place for people so framed! When life runs high and takes a common form men can walk together as the disciples walked on the road to Emmaus. Christian and Hopeful can pour out their hearts to one another as they travel towards the Celestial City and are knit together in everlasting bonds by the same Christ and the same salvation. But when each man is left to shift for himself, to work out the answers to his own problems, the result is isolation.

People who, if they were believers, would find the richest gift of life in utter confidence and mutual help are now necessarily strangers. One turns to metaphysics; another to science; one takes up with Rousseau's theory of existence, and another with Kant's; they meet; they have nothing to say; they are of no use to one another in trouble; one hears that the other is sick; what can be done? There is a nurse; he does not go; his old friend dies, and as to the funeral – well, we are liable to catch cold. Not so, Christian and Hopeful! for when Christian was troubled 'with apparitions of hobgoblins and evil spirits, even on the borderland of Heaven – oh, Bunyan! Hopeful kept his brother's head above water, and called upon him to turn his eyes to the Gate and the men standing by it to receive him.' My poor reader-friend, how many times have you in this nineteenth century, when the billows have gone over you – how many times have you felt the arm of man or woman under you raising you to see the shining ones and the glory that is inexpressible?

Had Catharine been born later it would have been better. She would perhaps have been able to distract herself with the thousand and one subjects which are now got up for examinations, or she would perhaps have seriously studied some science, which might at least have been effectual as an opiate in suppressing sensibility. She was, however, in Eastthorpe before the new education, as it is called, had been invented. There was no elaborate system of needle points, Roman and Greek history, plain and spherical trigonometry, political economy, ethics, literature, chemistry, conic sections, music, English history, and mental philosophy, to draw off the electricity within her, nor did she possess the invaluable privilege of being able, after studying a half-crown handbook, to unbosom herself to women of her own age upon the position of Longland as an English poet.

Shakespeare or Wordsworth might have been of some use to her, but to Shakespeare she was not led, although there was a brown, dusty, one-volume edition at the Terrace; and of Wordsworth nobody whom she knew in Eastthorpe had so much as heard. A book would have turned much that was vague in her into definite shape; it would have enabled her to recognise herself; it would have given an orthodox expression to cloudy singularity, and she would have seen that she was a part of humanity in her most extravagant and personal emotions. As it was, her position was critical because she stood by herself, affiliated to nothing, an individual belonging to no species, so far as she knew. She then met Mr Cardew. It was through him the word was spoken to her, and he was the interpreter of the new world to her. She was in love with him – but what is love? There is no such thing: there are loves, and they are all different. Catharine's was the very life of all that was Catharine, senses, heart, and intellect, a summing-up and projection of her whole selfhood. He was more to her than she to him – was any woman ever so much to a man as a man is to a woman? She was happy when she was near him. When she was in ordinary Eastthorpe society she felt as a pent-up lake might feel if the weight of its waters were used in threading needles, but when Mr Cardew talked to her, and she to him, she rejoiced in the flow of all her force, and that horrible oppression in her chest vanished.

Nevertheless, the fear, the shudder, came to her and not to him; the wrench came from her and not from him. It was she and not he who watched through the night and found no motive for the day, save a dull, miserable sense that it was her duty to live through it.

CHAPTER XI

It was a fact, and everybody noticed it, that since the removal to the Terrace, and the alteration in their way of living, Mr Furze was no longer the man he used to be, and seemed to have lost his grasp over his business. To begin with, he was not so much in the shop. His absences in the Terrace at meal-times made a great gap in the day, and Tom Catchpole was constantly left in sole charge. Mr Bellamy came home one evening and told his wife that he had called at Furze's to ask the meaning of a letter Furze had signed, explaining the action of a threshing-machine which was out of order. To his astonishment Furze, who was in his counting-house, called for Tom, and said, 'Here, Tom, this is one of your letters; you had better tell Mr Bellamy how the thing works.'

'I held my tongue, Mrs Bellamy, but I had my thoughts all the same, and the next time I go there, *if* I go at all, I shall ask for Tom.'

Mr Furze was aware of Tom's growing importance, and Mrs Furze was aware of it too. The worst of it was that Mr Furze, at any rate, knew that he could not do without him. It is very galling to the master to feel that his power is slipping from him into the hands of a subordinate, and he is apt to assert himself by spasmodic attempts at interference which generally make matters worse and rivet his chains more tightly. There was a small factory in Eastthorpe in which a couple of grindstones were used which were turned by water-power at considerable speed. One of them had broken at a flaw. It had flown to pieces while revolving, and had nearly caused a serious accident. The owner called at Mr Furze's to buy another. There were two in stock, one of which he would have taken; but Tom, his master being at the Terrace, strongly recommended his customer not to have that quality, as it was from the same quarry as the one which was faulty, but that another should be ordered. To this he assented. When Mr Furze returned Tom told him what had happened. He was in an unusually irritable, despotic mood. Mrs Furze had forced him to yield upon a point which he had foolishly made up his mind not to concede, and consequently he was all the more disposed to avenge his individuality elsewhere. After meditating for a minute or two he called Tom from the counter.

'Mr Catchpole, what do you mean by taking upon yourself to promise you would obtain another grindstone?'

'Mean, sir! I do not quite understand. The two out there are of the same sort as the one that broke, and I did not think them safe.'

'Think, sir! What business had you to think? I tell you what it is, you are much too fond of thinking. If you would only leave the thinking to me, and do what you are told, it would be much better for you.'

Tom's first impulse was to make a sharp reply, and to express his willingness to leave, but for certain private reasons he was silent. Encouraged by the apparent absence of resistance, Mr Furze continued –

'I've meant to have a word or two with you several times. You seem to have forgotten your position altogether, and that I am master here, and not you. You, perhaps, do not remember where you came from, and what you would have been if I had not picked you up. Let there be no misunderstanding in future.'

'There shall be none, sir. Shall I call at the factory and explain your wishes about the grindstone? I will tell them I was mistaken, and that they had better have one of those in stock.'

'No, you cannot do that now; let matters remain as they are; I must lose the sale of the stone and put up with it.'

Tom withdrew. That evening, after supper, Mr Furze, anxious to show his wife that he possessed some power to quell opposition, told her what had happened. It met with her entire approval. She hated Tom. For all hatred, as well as for all love, there is doubtless a reason, but the reasons for the hatreds of a woman of Mrs Furze's stamp are often obscure, and perhaps more nearly an exception than any other known fact in nature to the rule that every effect must have a cause.

'I would get rid of him,' said she. 'I think that his not replying to you is ten times more aggravating than if he had gone into a passion.'

'You cannot get rid of him,' said Catharine.

'Cannot! What do you mean, Catharine – cannot? I like that! Do you suppose that I do not understand my own business – I who took him up out of the gutter and taught him? Cannot, indeed!'

'Of course you *can* get rid of him, father; but I would not advise you to try it.'

'Now, do take *my* advice,' said Mrs Furze: 'send him about his business at once, before he does any further mischief, and gets hold of your connection. Promise me.'

'I will,' said Mr Furze, 'to-morrow morning, the very first thing.'

Morning came, and Mr Furze was not quite so confident. Mrs Furze had not relented, and as her husband went out at the door she reminded him of his vow.

'You will, now? I shall expect to hear when you come home that he has had notice.'

'Oh, certainly he shall go, but I am doubtful whether I had better not wait till I have somebody in my eye whom I can put in his place.'

'Nonsense! you can find somebody easily enough.'

Mr Furze strode into his shop looking and feeling very important. Instead of the usual kindly 'Good morning,' he nodded almost imperceptibly and marched straight into his counting-house. It had been his habit to call Tom in there and open the letters with him, Tom suggesting a course of action and replies. Today he opened his correspondence in silence. It happened to be unusually bulky for a small business, and unusually important. The Honourable Mr Eaton was about to make some important alterations in his house and grounds. New conservatories were to be built, and an elaborate system of hot water warming apparatus was to be put up both for house and garden. He had invited tenders to specification from three houses – one in London, one in Cambridge, and from Mr Furze. Tom and Mr Furze had gone over the specification carefully, but Tom had preceded and originated, and Mr Furze had followed, and, in order not to appear slow of comprehension, had frequently assented when he did not understand – a most dangerous weakness. To his surprise he found that his tender of £850 was accepted. There was much work to be done which was not in his line, but had been put into his contract in order to save subdivision, and consequently arrangements had to be made with sub-contractors. Materials had also to be provided at once, and there was a penalty of so much a day if the job was not completed by a certain time. He did not know exactly where to begin; he was stunned, as if somebody had hit him a blow on the head, and, after trying in vain to think, he felt that his brain was in knots. He put the thing aside, looked at his other letters, and they were worse. One of his creditors, a blacksmith, who owed him £55 for iron, had failed, and he was asked to attend a meeting of creditors. A Staffordshire firm, upon whom he had depended for pipes, in case he should obtain Mr Eaton's order, had sent a circular announcing an advance in iron, and he forgot that in their offer their price held good for another week. He was trustee under an old trust, upon which no action had been taken for years; he remembered none of its provisions, and now the solicitors had written to him requesting him to be present at a most important conference in London that day week. There was also a notice from the Navigation Commissioners informing him that, in consequence of an accident at one of their locks, it would be fully a fortnight before any barge could pass through, and he knew that his supply of smithery coal would be exhausted before that date, as he had refrained from purchasing in consequence of high prices. To crown everything a tap came at the door, and in walked his chief man at the foundry to announce that he would shortly leave, as he had obtained a better berth. Mr Furze by this time was so confused that he said nothing but 'Very well,' and when the man had gone he leaned his head on his elbows in despair. He looked through the glass window of the counting-house and saw Tom quietly weighing some nails. He would have given anything if he could have called him in, but he could not. As to dismissing him, it was out of the question now, and yet his sense of dependence on him excited a jealousy nearly as intense as his wife's animosity. When a man cannot submit to be helped he dislikes the benevolent friend who offers assistance worse than an avowed enemy. Mr Furze felt as if he must at once request Tom's aid, and at the same time do him some grievous bodily harm.

The morning passed away and nothing was advanced one single step. He went home to his dinner excited, and he was dangerous. It is very trying, when we are in a coil of difficulty, out of which we see no way of escape, to hear some silly thing suggested by an outsider who perhaps has not spent five minutes in considering the case. Mrs Furze, knowing nothing of Mr Eaton's contract, of the blacksmith's failure, of the advance in iron, of the trust meeting, of the stoppage of the navigation, and of the departure of the foundryman, asked her husband the moment the servant had brought in the dinner and had left the room –

'Well, my dear, what did Tom say when you told him to go?'

'I haven't told him.'

'Not told him, my dear! how is that?'

'I wish with all my heart you'd mind your own affairs.'

'Mr Furze! what is the matter? You do not seem to know what you are saying.'

'I know perfectly well what I am saying. I wish you knew what *you* are saying. When we came up here to the Terrace – much good has it done us – I thought I should have no interference with my business. You understand nothing whatever about it, and I shall take it as a favour if you will leave it alone.'

Mrs Furze was aghast. Presently she took out her pocket-handkerchief and retreated to her bedroom. Mr Furze did not follow her, but his dinner remained untouched. When he rose to leave, Catharine went after him to the door, caught hold of his hand and silently kissed him, but he did not respond.

During the dinner-hour Tom had looked in the counting-house and saw the letters lying on the table untouched. Mr Eaton's steward came in with congratulations that the tender was accepted, but he could not wait. As Mr Furze passed through the shop Tom told him simply that the steward had called.

'What did he want?'

'I do not know, sir.'

Mr Furze went to his papers again and shut the door. He was still more incapable of collecting his thoughts and of determining how to begin. First of all came the contract, but before he could settle a single step the navigation presented itself. Then, without any progress, came the rise in the price of iron, and so forth. In about three hours the post would be going, and nothing was done. He cast about for some opportunity of a renewal of intercourse with Tom, and looked anxiously through his window, hoping that Tom might have some question to ask. At last he could stand it no longer, and he opened the door and called out –

'Mr Catchpole' – not the familiar 'Tom'.

Mr Catchpole presented himself.

'I wish to give you some instructions about these letters. I have arranged them in order. You will please write what I say, and I will sign in time for the post tonight. First of all there is the contract. You had better take the necessary action and ask the Staffordshire people what advance they want.'

'Yes, sir, but' – deferentially – 'the Staffordshire people cannot claim an advance if you accept at once: you remember the condition?'

'Certainly; what I mean is that you can accept their tender. Then there is the meeting of creditors.'

'I suppose you wish Mr Eaton's acceptance acknowledged and the sub-contractors at once informed?'

'Of course, of course; I said necessary action – that covers everything. With regard to the creditors' meeting, my proposal is – ' A pause.

'Perhaps it will be as well, sir, if you merely say you will attend.'

'I thought you would take that for granted. I was considering what proposal I should make when we meet.'

'Probably, sir, you can make it better after you hear his statement.'

'Well, possibly it may be so; but I am always in favour of being prepared. However, we will postpone that for the present.

Then there is the trustee business. That is a private matter of my own, which you will not understand. I will give you the papers, however, and you can make an abstract of them. I cannot carry every point in my head. If you are in any doubt come to me.'

'You wish me to say you will go, sir?'

'I should have thought there was no need to ask. You surely do not suppose that I am to give instructions upon every petty detail! Then about the navigation: I *must* have some coal, and that is the long and the short of it.'

The 'how' was probably a petty detail, for Mr Furze went no further with the subject, and was inclined to proceed with the man at the foundry.

'It will be too late if we wait till the lock is repaired, sir. I understand it will be three weeks really. Will you write to Ditchfield and tell them five tons are to come to Millfield Sluice? We will then cart it from there. That will be the cheapest and the best way.'

'Yes, I do not object; but we *must* have the coal – that is really the important point. As to Jack in the foundry, I will get somebody else. I suppose we shall have to pay more.'

'How would it be, sir, if you put Sims in Jack's place, and Spurling in Sims' place? You would then only want a new labourer, and you would pay no more than you pay now. Sims, too, knows the work, and it might be awkward to have a new man at the head just now.'

'Yes, that may do; but what I wish to impress on you is that the vacancy *must* be filled up. That is all, I think; you can take the letters.'

Tom took them up and went to his little corner near the window to re-peruse them. There was much to be done which had not been mentioned, particularly with regard to Mr Eaton's contract. He took out the specification, jotted down on a piece of paper the several items, marked methodically with a cross those which required prompt attention, and began to write. Mr Furze, seeing his desk unencumbered, was very well satisfied with himself. He had 'managed' the whole thing perfectly. His head became clear, the knots were untied, and he hummed a few bars of a hymn. He then went to his safe, took out the trust papers without looking at them, handed them over to Tom with a remark that he should like the abstract the next morning, and at once went up to the Terrace. He was hungry: he had left Mrs Furze unwell, and, in his extreme good-humour, had relented towards her. She had recovered, but did not mention again the subject of Tom's discharge. He had ham with his tea, but it was over sooner than usual, and he rose to depart.

'You are going early, father,' said Catharine.

'Yes, my dear; it has been a busy day. I have been successful with my tender for Mr Eaton's improvements; iron has advanced; the navigation has stopped; Castle, the blacksmith, has gone to smash; I have to go to a trustees' meeting under that old Fothergill trust; and Jack in the foundry has given notice to leave.'

'When did you hear all this?'

'All within an hour after breakfast. I have been entirely occupied this afternoon in directing Tom what to do, and I must be off to see that he has carried out my instructions. What a coil it is! and yet I rather like it.'

Catharine reflected that her father did not seem to like it at dinner-time, and went through the familiar operation of putting two and two together. She accompanied him to the front gate, and as he passed out she said –

'You have not given Tom notice?'

'No, my dear, not yet. It would be a little inconvenient at present. I *could* do without him easily, even now; but perhaps it will be better to wait. Besides, he is a little more teachable after the talking-to I have given him.'

Mr Furze signed his letters. He did not observe that many others, of which he had not thought, remained to be written, and when Tom brought them the next day he made no remark. The assumption was that he had noticed the day before what remained to be done, saw that it was not urgent, and consented to the delay. The curious thing was that he assumed it to himself. It is a fact – not incredible to those who know that nobody, not the most accomplished master in flattery, can humbug us so completely as we can and do humbug ourselves – that Mr Furze, ten minutes after the letters were posted, was perfectly convinced that he had foreseen the necessity of each one – that he had personally and thoroughly controlled the whole day's operations, and that Tom had performed the duties of a merely menial clerk. As he went home he thought over Catharine's attitude with regard to Tom. She, in reality, had been anxious to protect her father; but such a motive he could not be expected to suggest to himself. A horrid notion came into his head. She might be fond of Tom! Did she not once save his life? Had she not, even when a child, pleaded that something ought to be done for him? Had she not affirmed that he was indispensable? Had she not inquired again about him that very day? Had she not openly expressed her contempt for that most eligible person, Mr Colston? He determined to watch most strictly, and again he resolved to dismiss his assistant. A trifling increase in his attention to small matters would enable him to do this within a month or two. It would be as well for Mrs Furze to watch too. After supper Catharine went to bed early, and her father hung out the white flag, to which friendly response was given directly the subject of his communications was apparent. It became a basis of almost instantaneous reconciliation, and Mrs Furze, mindful of the repulse of the brewer's son and the ruin of her own scheme thereon built, hated Tom more than ever. It was Tom, then, who had prevented admission into Eastthorpe society.

CHAPTER XII

Mr Tom Catchpole had never had any schooling. What he had learned he had learned by himself, and the books he had read were but few, and chosen rather by chance. He had never had the advantage of the common introduction to the world of ideas which is given, in a measure, to all boys who are systematically taught by teachers, and consequently, not knowing the relative value of what came before him, his perspective and proportion were incorrect. His mind, too, was essentially plain. He was perfect in his loyalty to duty; he was, as we have seen, very good in business matters, had a clear head, and could give shrewd advice upon any solid matter-of-fact difficulty, but the spiritual world was non-existent for him. He attended chapel regularly, for he was a Dissenter, but his reasons for going, so far as he had any, were very simple. There was a great God in heaven, against whom he had sinned and was perpetually sinning. To save himself from the consequences of his transgressions certain means were provided, and he was bound to use them. On Monday morning chapel and all thoughts connected with it entirely disappeared, but he said his prayers twice a day with great regularity. There are very few, however, of God's creatures to whom the supernatural does not in some way present itself, and no man lives by bread alone. To Tom, Catharine was miracle, soul, inspiration, religion, enthusiasm, patriotism, immortality, the fact, essentially identical, whatever we like to call it, which is not bread and yet is life. He never dared to say anything to her. He felt that she lived in a world beyond him, and he did not know what kind of a world it was. He knew that she thought about things which were strange to him, and that she was anxious upon subjects which never troubled him. She was often greatly depressed when there was no cause for depression, so far as he could see, and he could not comprehend why a person should be ill when there was nothing the matter. If he felt unwell – a rare event with him – he always took two antibilious pills before going to bed, and was all right the next morning. He wished he himself could be ill without a reason, and then perhaps he would be able to understand Catharine better. Her elation and excitement were equally unintelligible. He once saw her sitting in her father's counting-house with a book. She was not a great reader – nobody in Eastthorpe read books, and there were not many to read – but she was so absorbed in this particular book that she did not lift her eyes from it when he came in, and it was not until her father had spoken twice to her, and had told her that he was expecting somebody, that she moved. She then ran upstairs into a store-room, and was there for half an hour in the cold. The book was left open when she went away, and Tom looked at it. It was a collection of poems by all kinds of people, and the one over which she had been poring was about a man who had shot an albatross. Tom studied it, but could make nothing of it, and yet this was what had so much interested her! 'O God!' he said to himself, passionately, 'if I could, if I did but know! She cares not a pin for me; this is what she cares for.' Poor Tom! he did not pride himself on the absence of a sense in him, but knew and acknowledged to himself that he was defective. It is quite possible to be aware of a spiritual insensibility which there is no power to overcome – of the existence of a universe in which other favoured souls are able to live, one which they can report, and yet its doors are closed to us, or, if sitting outside we catch a glimpse of what is within, we have no power to utter a single sufficient word to acquaint anybody with what we have seen. Catharine respected Tom greatly, for she understood well enough what her father owed to him, but she could not love him. One penetrating word from Mr Cardew thrilled every fibre in her, no matter what the subject might be. Tom, in every mood and on every topic, was uninteresting and ordinary. To tell the truth, plain, common probity taken by itself was not attractive to her. Horses, dogs, cows, the fields were more stimulant than perfect integrity, for she was young and did not know how precious it was; but, after all, the reason of reasons why she did not love Tom was that she did not love him.

It was announced one day by small handbills in the shop windows that a sermon was to be preached by Mr Cardew, of Abchurch, in Eastthorpe, on behalf of the County Infirmary, and Catharine went to hear him. It was in the evening, and she was purposely late. She did not go to her mother's pew, but sat down close to the door. To her surprise she saw Tom not far off. He was on his way to his chapel, when he noticed Catharine alone, walking towards the church, and he had followed her. Mr Cardew took for his text the parable of the prodigal son. He began by saying that this parable had been taken to be an exhibition of God's love for man. It seemed rather intended to set forth, not the magnificence of the Divine nature, but of human nature – of that nature which God assumed. The determination on the part of the younger son to arise, to go to his father, and above everything to say to him simply 'Father, I have sinned,' was as great as God is great: it was God – God moving in us; in a sense it was far more truly God – far greater than the force which binds the planets into a system. But the splendour of human nature – do not suppose any heresy here; it is Bible truth, the very gospel – is shown in the father as well as in the son. 'When he was yet a great way off.' We are as good as told, then, that day after day the father had been watching. How small were the probabilities that at any particular hour the son would return, and yet every hour the father's eyes were on that long, dusty road! When at last he saw what he was dying to see, what did he say? Was there a word of rebuke? He stopped his boy's mouth with kisses, and cried for the best robe and the ring and the shoes, and proclaimed a feast – the ring, mark you, a sign of honour!

> 'Say nothing of pardon; the darkness hath gone:
> Shall pardon be asked for the night by the sun?
> No word of the past; of the future no fear:
> 'Tis enough, my beloved, to know thou art here.'

'Oh, my friends,' said the preacher, 'just consider that it is this upon which Jesus, the Son of God, has put His stamp, not the lecture, not chastisement, not expiation, but an instant unquestioning embrace, no matter what the wrong may have been. If you say this is dangerous doctrine, I say it is *here*. What other meaning can you give to it? At the same time I am astonished to find it here, astonished that priestcraft and the enemy of souls should not have erased it. Sacred truth! Is it not moving to think of all the millions of men who for eighteen hundred years have read this parable, philosophers and peasants, in every climate, and now are we reading it to-day! Is it not moving – nay, awful – to think of all the good it has done, of the sweet stream of tenderness, broad and deep, which has flowed down from it through all history? History would have been different if this parable had never been told.'

Mr Cardew paused, and after his emotion had a little subsided he concluded by an appeal on behalf of the infirmary. He inserted a saving clause on Christ's mediatorial work, but it had no particular connection with the former part of his discourse. It was spoken in a different tone, and it satisfied the congregation that they had really heard nothing heterodox.

Tom watched Catharine closely. He noted her eager, rapt attention, and that she did not recover herself till the voluntary was at an end. He went out after her; she met Mr and Mrs Cardew at the churchyard gates; he saw the excitement of all three, and he saw Catharine leave her friends at the Rectory, for they were evidently going to stay the night there. Mrs Cardew went into the house first, but Catharine turned down Fosbrooke Street, a street which did not lead, save by a very roundabout way, to the Terrace. Presently Mr Cardew came out and walked slowly down Rectory Lane. In those days it was hardly a thoroughfare. It ended at the river bank, and during daylight a boat was generally there, belonging to an old, superannuated boatman, who carried chance passengers over to the mill meadows and saved them a walk if they wanted to go that side of the town. A rough seat had been placed near the boat moorings for the convenience of the ferryman's customers. At this time in the evening the place was deserted. Tom followed Mr Cardew, and presently overtook him. Mr Cardew and he knew one another slightly, for there were few persons for miles round who did not now and then visit Mr Furze's shop.

'Good evening, Mr Cardew.'

'Ah! Mr Catchpole, is that you? What are you doing here?'

'I have been to hear you preach, sir, and I thought I would have a stroll before I went home.'

'I thought I should like a stroll too.'

The two went on together, and sat down on the seat. The moon had just risen, nearly full, sending its rays obliquely across the water, and lighting up the footpath which went right and left along the river's edge. Mr Cardew seemed disinclined to talk, was rather restless, and walked backwards and forwards by the bank. Tom reflected that he might be intruding, but there was something on his mind, and he did not leave. Mr Cardew sat down again by his side. They both happened to be looking in the same direction eastwards at the same moment.

'If that lady thinks to cross tonight,' said Tom, 'she's mistaken. I'd take her over myself, though it is Sunday, if the boat were not locked.'

'What lady?' asked Mr Cardew – as if he were frightened, Tom thought.

'The lady coming down there just against the willow.'

Mr Cardew was short-sighted, and could not see her. He made as if he would go to meet her, but he stopped, returned, and remained standing. The figure approached, but before Tom could discern anything more than that it was a woman, it disappeared behind the hedge up the little by-path that cut off the corner into Rectory Lane.

'She's gone,' said Tom. 'I suppose she was not coming here after all.'

'Which way has she gone?' asked Mr Cardew, looking straight on the ground and scratching it with his stick.

'Into the town.'

'I must be going, I think, Mr Catchpole; good-night.'

'I'll walk with you as far as your door, sir. There's something I want to say to you.'

Mr Cardew did not reply, and meditated for a moment.

'It is a lovely evening. We will sit here a little longer. What is it?'

'Mr Cardew, as I said, I have been to hear you preach, and I thank you with all my heart for your sermon, but I want to ask you something about it. What you said about the Mediator was true enough, but somehow, sir, I feel as if I ought to have liked the first part most, but I couldn't, and perhaps the reason is that it was poetry. Oh, Mr Cardew, if you could but tell me how to like poetry!'

'I am afraid neither I nor anybody else can teach you that; but why are you anxious to like it? Why are you dissatisfied with yourself?'

'I do not think I am stupid. When I am in the shop I know that I am more than a match for most persons, and yet, Mr Cardew, there are some people who seem to me to have something I have not got, and they value it more than anything besides, and they have nothing to say really, *really*, I mean, to those who have not got it, although they are kind to them.'

'It is not very easy to understand what you mean.'

'Well, now tonight, sir, when you talked about God moving in us, and the force which binds the planets together, and all that, I am sure you felt it, and I am sure it is true, and yet I was out of doors, so to speak.'

'Perhaps I may be peculiar, and it is you who are sane and sound.'

'Ah, Mr Cardew, if you were alone in it, and everybody were like me, that might be true, but it is not so; it is I who am alone.'

'Who cares for it whom you know? You are under a delusion.'

'Oh, no, I am not. Why there – there.' Tom stopped.

'There was what?'

'There was Miss Furze – she took it in.'

'Indeed!' Mr Cardew again looked straight on the ground, and again scratched it with his stick. It was a night of nights, dying twilight long lingering in the north-west, the low golden moon, the slow, placid, shining stream, perfect stillness. Tom was not very susceptible, but even he was overcome and tempted into confidence.

'Mr Cardew, you are a minister, and I may tell you: I know you will not betray me. I love Miss Furze; I cannot help it. I have never loved any girl before. It is very foolish, for I am only her father's journeyman; but that might be got over. She would not let that stand in her way, I am sure. But, Mr Cardew, I am not up to her; she is strange to me. If I try to mention her subjects, what I say is not right, and when I drove her home from Chapel Farm, and admired the view I know she admired, she directly began to speak about business, as if she did not wish to talk about better things; perhaps it is because I never was taught. I had no schooling; cannot you help me, sir? I shall never set eyes on anybody like her. I would die this instant to save her a moment's pain.'

Mr Cardew was silent. It was characteristic of him that often when he himself was most personally affected, the situation became an object of reflection. What a strange pathos there was in this recognition of superiority and in the inability to rise to it and appropriate it! Then his thoughts turned to himself again, and the flame shot up clear and strong, as if oil had been poured on the fire. She understood him; she alone.

'I am very sorry for you, Mr Catchpole, more sorry than I can tell you. I will think over what you have said, and we will have another talk about it. I must be going now.'

Mr Cardew, however, did not go towards Rectory Lane, but along the side path. Tom mechanically accompanied him, but without speaking. At last Mr Cardew, finding that Tom did not leave him, retraced his steps and went up the lane. In about two minutes they met Mrs Cardew.

'I wondered where you were. I was coming down to the ferry to look for you, thinking that most likely you were there. Ah, Mr Catchpole! is that you? I am glad my husband has had company. Let me go back and look at the water.'

'Certainly.'

Tom stopped and took his leave.

The two went back to the river and sat on the seat.

Mrs Cardew took her husband's hand in her own sweet way, kissed it, and held it fast. At last, with a little struggle, she said –

'My dear, you have never preached – to me, at least – as you have preached tonight.'

'You really mean it?'

She kissed his hand again, and leaned her head on his shoulder. That was her reply. He clasped her tenderly, fervently, more than fervently, and yet! while his mouth was on her neck, and his arms were round her body, the face of Catharine presented itself, and it was not altogether his wife whom he caressed.

Meanwhile Tom, pursuing his way homewards, overtook Miss Furze, to his great surprise.

'Tom, where have you been?'

'I have just left Mr and Mrs Cardew.'

Catharine, on her way home, hesitating – for it was Catharine whom Tom and Mr Cardew saw – had met Mrs Cardew just about to leave the house.

'Why, Catharine! you here?'

'I was tempted by the night.'

'Catharine, did you ever hear my husband preach better than he did to-night?'

'Never!'

'I was so proud of him, and I was so happy, because just what touched him touched me too. Come back with me: I know he has gone to the ferry.'

'No, thank you; it is late.'

'I am sure he will see you home.'

'I am sure he shall not. What! walk up to the Terrace after a day's hard work!'

So they parted. What had passed between Catharine and Mr Cardew when they lingered behind at the Rectory gate, God and they only know, but what we call an accident prevented their meeting. Accident! my friend Reuben told me the other day his marriage was an accident. The more I think about accidents, the less do I believe in them. By chance he had an invitation to go to Shott Woods one afternoon, and there he saw the girl who afterwards became his wife and the mother of children with a certain stamp upon them. They in turn will have other children, all of them moulded after a fashion which would have been difficult if his wife had been another woman. Nay, *these* children would not have existed if this particular marriage had not taken place. Thus the whole course of history is altered, because of that little note and a casual encounter. But, putting aside the theory of a God who ordains results absolutely inevitable, although to us it seems as if they might have been different, it may be observed that the attraction which drew Reuben to his dear Camilla was not quite fortuitous. What decided her to go? It was perfect autumn weather; it was just the time of year she most loved; there would be no crowding or confusion, for many people had gone away to the seaside, and so she was delighted at the thought of the picnic. What decided him to go? The very same reasons. They had both been to Shott during the season, and he had talked and laughed there with some delightful creatures before she crossed his path and held him for ever. Why had he waited? Why had she waited? We have discarded Providence as our forefathers believed in it; but nevertheless there is a providence without the big P, if we choose so to spell it, and yet surely deserving it as much as the Providence of theology, a non-theological Providence which watches over us and lead us. It appears as instinct prompting us to do this and not to do that, to decide this way or that way when we have no consciously rational ground for decision, to cleave to this person and shun the other, almost before knowing anything of either: it has been recognised in all ages under various forms as Demon, Fate, or presiding Genius. But still further. Suppose they both went to Shott Woods idly; suppose – which was not the case – they had never heard of one another before, is it not possible that they were brought together by a law as unevadable as gravity? There would be nothing more miraculous in such attraction than there is in that thread which the minutest atom of gas in the Orion nebula extends across billions of miles to the minutest atom of dust on the road under my window. However, be all this as it may, it would be wrong to say that the meeting between Catharine and Mr Cardew was prevented by accident. She loitered: she went up Fosbrooke Street: if she had gone straight to Mr Cardew she might have been with him before Tom met him. Tom would not have interrupted them, for he ventured to speak to Mr Cardew merely because he was alone, and Mrs Cardew would not have interrupted them, for they would have gone further afield. Tom's appearance even was not an accident, but a thread carefully woven, one may say, in the web that night.

'I saw you at church tonight, Miss Catharine,' said Tom, as they walked homewards.

'Why did you go? You do not usually go to church.'

'I thought I should like to hear Mr Cardew, and I am very glad I went.'

'Are you? What did you think of him? Did you like him?'

'Oh, yes; it was all true; but what he said about Christ the Mediator was so clearly put.'

'You did not care for the rest then?'

'I did indeed, Miss Catharine, but it is just the same with our minister: I get along with him so much better when he seems to follow the catechism, but' – he looked up in her face – 'I know that is not what you cared for. Oh, Miss Catharine,' he cried suddenly, and quite altering his voice and manner, 'I do not know when I shall have another chance; I hardly dare tell you; you won't spurn me, will you? My father was a poor workman; I was nothing better, and should have been nothing better if it had not been for you; all my schooling almost I have done myself; I know nothing compared with what you know; but, Miss Catharine, I love you to madness: I have loved no woman but you; never looked at one, I may say. Do you remember when you rode home with me from Chapel Farm? I have lived on it ever since. You are far above me: things come and speak to you which I don't see. If you would teach me I should soon see them too.'

Catharine was silent, and perfectly calm. At last she said –

'My dear Tom.'

Tom shuddered at the tone.

'No, Miss Catharine, don't say it now; think a little; don't cast me off in a moment.'

'My dear Tom, I may as well say it now, for what I ought to say is as clear as that moon in the sky. I can *never* love you as a wife ought to love her husband.'

'Oh, Miss Catharine! you despise me, you despise me! Why in God's name?' Tom rose above himself, and became such another self that Catharine was amazed and half staggered. 'Why in God's name did He make you and me after such a fashion, that you are the one person in the world able to save me, and you cannot! Why did He do this! Why did He put me where I saw you every day and torment me with the hope of you, knowing that you would have nothing to do with me! He maimed my father and made him a beggar: He prevented me from learning what would have made me fit for you, and then He drove me to worship you. Do not say "never"!'

They were close to her father's door at the Terrace. She stopped, looked at him sadly, but decisively, straight in the face, and said –

'Never! never! Never your lover, but your best friend for ever,' and she opened the gate and disappeared.

CHAPTER XIII

Mr and Mrs Furze were not disturbed because their daughter was late. A neighbour told them that she had gone to the Rectory with Mr and Mrs Cardew, and Mrs Furze was pleased that Eastthorpe should behold her daughter apparently on intimate terms with a clergyman so well known and so respectable. But it was ten o'clock, and they wished to be in bed. Mrs Furze had gone to the window, and had partly pushed aside the blind, watching till Catharine should appear. Just as the clock struck she saw Catharine approaching with somebody whom she of course took for Mr Cardew. The pair came nearer, and, to her astonishment, she recognised Tom. Nay more, she saw the couple halt near the gate, and that Tom was speaking very earnestly. Mrs Furze was so absorbed that she did not recover herself until the interview was at an end, and before she could say a word to her husband, who was asleep in the armchair, her daughter was at the door. Mrs Furze went to open it.

'Why, Catharine, that surely wasn't Tom!'

'Yes, it was, mother. Why not?'

'To-om!' half shrieked Mrs Furze.

'Yes, Tom: I suppose father has gone to bed? Good-night mother,' and Catharine kissed her on the forehead and went upstairs.

Mrs Furze shut the door and rushed into the room.

'My dear! my dear!' shaking him, 'Catharine has come, and Tom brought her, and they stood ever so long talking to one another.'

Mr Furze roused himself and took a little brandy-and-water.

'Rubbish!'

'Rubbish! it's all very well for you to say rubbish when you've been snoring there.'

'Well, where is she? Make her come in; let us hear what she

116

has to say.'

'She's gone to bed. Now take my advice: don't speak to her tonight, but wait till tomorrow; you know what she is, and you had better think a bit.'

Mrs Furze, notwithstanding her excitement, dreaded somewhat attacking Catharine without preparation.

'There's no mistake about it,' observed Mr Furze, rousing himself, 'that I have had my suspicions of Master Tom, but I never thought it would come to this; nor that Catharine would have anything to say to him. It was she, though, who said I could not do without him.'

'It was she,' added Mrs Furze, 'who always stuck out against our coming up here, and was rude to Mrs Colston and her son. I do not blame her so much, though, as I do that wretch of a Catchpole. What he wants is plain enough: he'll marry her and have the business, the son of a blind beggar who used to go on errands! Oh me! to think it has come to this, that my only child should be the wife of a pauper's son, and we've struggled so hard! What will the Colstons say, and all the church folk, and all the town, for the matter of that!'

Here Mrs Furze threw herself down in a chair and became hysterical. Poor woman! she really cared for Catharine, loved her in a way, and was horrified for her sake at the supposed engagement, but her desire for her daughter's welfare was bound up with a desire for her own, a strand of one interlaced with a strand of the other, so that they could not be separated. It might be said that the union of the two impulses was even more intimate, that it was like a mixture of two liquids. There was no conflict in her. She was not selfish at one moment, and unselfishly anxious for her child the next; but she was both together at the same instant, the particular course on which she might determine satisfying both instincts.

Mr Furze unfastened his wife's gown and staylaces and gave her a stimulant. Presently, after directing him with a gasp to open the window, she recovered herself.

'I'll discharge Mr Tom at once,' said her husband, 'and tell him the reason.'

'Now, don't be stupid, Furze; pull down that blind, will you?

Fancy leaving it up, and the moon staring straight down upon me half undressed! Don't you admit anything of the kind to Tom. I would not let him believe you could suspect it. Besides, if you were to dismiss him for such a reason as that, you would make Catharine all the more obstinate, and the whole town would hear of it, and we should perhaps be laughed at, and lots of people would take Tom's part and say we might go further and fare worse, and were stuck up, and all that, for we must remember that all the Furzes were of humble origin, and Eastthorpe knows it. No, no, we will get rid of Tom, but it shall not be because of Catharine – something better than that – you leave it to me.'

'Well, how about Catharine?'

'We will have her in tomorrow morning, when we are not so flurried. I always like to talk to her just after breakfast if there is anything wrong; but do not say a word to Tom.'

Mrs Furze took another sip of the brandy-and-water and went to bed. Mr Furze shut the window, mixed a little more brandy-and-water, and, as he drank it, reflected deeply. Most vividly did that morning come back to him when he had once before decided to eject Mr Catchpole.

'I do not know how it is with other people,' he groaned, 'but whenever I have settled on a thing something is sure to turn up against it, and I never know what to be at for the best. My head, too, is not quite what it used to be. Half a dozen worries at once do muddle me. If they would but come, one up and one down, nobody could beat me.' He took another sip of the brandy-and-water. 'Want of practice – that's all. I have been an idiot to let him do so much. He shall go;' and Mr Furze put out the candles.

Catharine was down before either her father or mother, and stood at the window reading when her father came in. She bade him good morning and kissed him, but he was ill at ease, and pretended to look for something on the side-table. He felt he was not sufficiently supported by the main strength of his forces; he was afraid to speak, and he retreated to his bedroom, sitting down disconsolately on a rush-bottom chair whilst his wife dressed herself.

'She's there already,' he said.

'Then it is as well you came back.'

'I think you had better begin with her; you are her mother, and we will wait till breakfast is over. Perhaps she will say something to us. How had we better set about it?'

'I shall ask her straight what she means.'

'How shall we go on then?'

'How shall we go on then? What! won't *you* have a word to put in about her marrying a fellow like that, your own servant with such a father? And how are they to live, pray? Am I to have him up here to tea with us, and is Phœbe to answer the front door when they knock, and is she to wait upon him, *him* who always goes down the area steps to the kitchen? I do not believe Phœbe would stop a month, for with all her faults she does like a respectable family. And then, if they go to church, are they to have our pew, and is Mrs Colston to call on me and say, "How is Catharine, and how is your *son-in-law*?" And then – oh dear, oh dear! – is his father to come here too, and is Catharine to bring him, and is he to be at the wedding breakfast? And perhaps Mrs Colston will inquire after him too. But there, I shall not survive *that*! Oh! Catharine, Catharine!'

Mrs Furze dropped on the chair opposite the looking-glass, for she was arranging her back hair while this monologue was proceeding, although the process was interrupted here and there when her emotions got the better of her. Her hair fell into confusion again, and it seemed as if she would again be upset even at that early hour. Her husband gave her a smelling-bottle, and she slowly recommenced her toilette.

'Would it not,' he said, 'be as well to try and soften her a bit, and remind her of her duty to her parents?'

'You might finish up with that, but I don't believe she'd care; and what are we to do if she owns it all and sticks out – that's what I want to know?'

Mr Furze was silent.

'There you sit, Furze; you *are* provoking! Pick up that hairpin, will you? You always sit and sit whenever there's any difficulty. You never go beyond what I have in my own head, and when I *do* stir you up to think it is sure to be something of no use.'

'I'll do anything you want,' said the pensive husband, as his wife rose and put on her cap. 'I've told you before I'll get rid of Tom, and then perhaps it will all come round!'

'At it again! What *did* I tell you last night? – and yet you go on with your old tune. All come round, indeed! Would it! She's your daughter, but you don't know her as I do.'

Here there came a tap at the door. It was Phœbe: Miss Catharine sent her to say it was a quarter-past eight: should she make the coffee?

'Look at that!' said Mrs Furze: 'shall she make the coffee! – after what has happened! That's the kind of girl she is. It strikes me you had better have nothing to do with her and leave her to me.'

Phœbe tapped again.

'Certainly not,' replied Mrs Furze. 'I'll begin,' she added to her husband, 'by letting her know that at least I am not dead.'

'Well, we'd better go. You just tackle her, and I'll chime in.'

The couple descended, but their plan of campaign was not very clearly elaborated, and even the one or two lines of assault which Mrs Furze had prepared turned out to be useless. It is all very well to decide what is to be done with a human being if the human being will but comport himself in a fairly average manner, but if he will not the plan is likely to fail.

Mr Furze was very restless during his meal. He went to the window two or three times, and returned with the remark that it was going to be wet; but the observation was made in a low, mumbling tone. Mrs Furze was also fidgety, and, in reply to her daughter's questions, complained of headache, and wondered that Catharine could not see that she had had no sleep. At last the storm broke.

'Catharine,' said Mrs Furze, 'it *was* Tom, then, who came home with you last night.'

'It was Tom, mother.'

'Tom! What do you mean, child? How – how did he – where did you meet him?'

Mr Furze retired from the table, where the sun fell full upon him, and sat in the easy-chair, where he was more in the shade.

'He overtook me somewhere near the Rectory.'

'Now, Catharine, don't answer your mother like that,' interposed Mr Furze; 'you know what you heard, or might have heard, last Sunday morning, that prevarication is very much like a lie; why don't you speak out the truth?'

Catharine was silent for a moment.

'I have answered exactly the question mother asked.'

'Catharine, you know perfectly well what I mean,' said Mrs Furze; 'what is the use of pretending you do not! Tom would never dare to walk with you in a public street, and at night, too, if there were not something more than you like to say. Tom Catchpole! whose father sold laces on the bridge; and to think of all we have done for you, and the money we have spent on you, and the pains we have taken to bring you up respectably! I will not say anything about religion, and all that, for I daresay that is nothing to *you*, but you might have had some consideration for your mother, especially in her weak state of health, before you broke her heart, and yet I blame myself, for you always had low tastes – going to Bellamy's, and consorting with people of that kind rather than with your mother's friends. Do you suppose Mrs Colston will come near us again! And it all comes to trying to do one's best, for there's Carry Hawkins, only a grocer's daughter, who never had a sixpence spent on her compared with what you have, and she is engaged to Carver, the doctor at Cambridge. Oh, it's a serpent's tooth, it is, and if we had never scraped and screwed for you, and denied ourselves, but left you to yourself, you might have been better; oh dear, oh dear!'

Catharine held her tongue. She saw instantly that if she denied any engagement with Tom she would not be believed, and that in any case Tom would have to depart. Moreover, one of her defects was a certain hardness to persons for whom she had small respect, and she did not understand that just because Mrs Furze was her mother she owed her at least a deference, and, if possible, a tenderness due to no other person. However weak, foolish, and even criminal parents may be, a child ought to honour them as Moses commanded, for the injunction is, and should be, entirely unconditional.

'Catharine,' said Mr Furze, 'why do you not answer your mother?'

'I cannot; I had better leave.'

She opened the door and went to her room. After she had left further debate arose, and three points were settled: First, that no opposition should be offered to a visit to Chapel Farm, which had been proposed for the next day, as she would be better at the Farm than at the Terrace; secondly, that Tom and she were in love with one another; and thirdly, that not a word should be said to Tom. 'Leave that to me,' said Mrs Furze again. Although she saw nothing distinctly, a vague, misty hope dawned upon her, the possibility of something she could not yet discern, and, notwithstanding the blow she had received, she was decidedly more herself within an hour after breakfast than she had been during the twelve hours preceding.

CHAPTER XIV

In Mr Furze's establishment was a man who went by the name of Orkid Jim, 'Orkid' signifying the general contradictoriness and awkwardness of his temper. He had a brother who was called Orkid Joe, in the employ of a builder in the town, but it was the general opinion that Orkid Jim was much the orkider of the two. He was a person with whom Mr Furze seldom interfered. He was, it is true, a good workman in the general fitting department, in setting grates, and for jobs of that kind, but he was impertinent and disobedient. Mr Furze, however, tolerated his insults, and generally allowed him to have his own way. He was not afraid of Orkid Jim, but he was a victim to that unhappy dread of a quarrel which is the torment and curse of weak minds. It is, no doubt, very horrible to see a man trample upon opinions and feelings as easily and carelessly as he would upon the grass, and go on his way undisturbed, but it is more painful to see faltering, trembling incapacity for self-assertion, especially before subordinates. Mr Furze could not have suffered more than two or three days' inconvenience if Orkid Jim had been discharged, but a vague terror haunted him of something which might possibly happen. Partly this distressing weakness is due to the absence of a clear conviction that we are right; it is an intellectual difficulty; but frequently it is simple mushiness of character, the same defect which tempts us, when we know a thing is true, to whittle it down if we meet with opposition, and to refrain from presenting it in all its sharpness. Cowardice of this kind is not only injustice to ourselves, but to our friends. We inflict a grievous wrong by compromise. We are responsible for what we see, and the denial or the qualification should be left to take care of itself. Our duty is, if possible, to give a distinct outline to what we have in our mind. It is easy to say we should not be obstinate, pig-headed, and argue for argument's sake. That is true, just as much as every half truth is true, but the other half is also true.

Mr Furze, excepting when he was out of temper, never stood up to Orkid Jim. He needed the stimulus of passion to do what ought to have been done by reason, and when we cannot do what is right save under the pressure of excitement it is generally misdone. Orkid Jim had a great dislike to Tom, which he took no pains to conceal. It was difficult to ascertain the cause, but partly it was jealousy. Tom had got before him. This, however, was not all. It was a case of pure antipathy, such as may often be observed amongst animals. Some dogs are the objects of special hatred by others, and are immediately attacked by them, before any cause of offence can possibly have been given.

Jim had called at the Terrace on the morning after the explosion with Catharine. He came to replace a cracked kitchen boiler, and Mrs Furze, for some reason or other, felt inclined to go down into the kitchen and have some talk with him. She knew how matters stood between him and Tom.

'Well, Jim, how are you getting on now? I have not seen you lately.'

'No, marm, I ain't one as comes to the front much now.'

'What do you mean? I suppose you might if you liked. I am sure Mr Furze values you highly.'

Jim was cautious and cunning; not inclined to commit himself. He consequently replied by an 'Ah,' and knocked with great energy at the brickwork from which he was detaching the range.

'Anything been the matter, then, Jim?'

'No, marm; nothing's the matter.'

'You have not quarrelled with Mr Furze, I hope? You do not seem quite happy.'

'Me quarrel with Mr Furze, marm! – no, I never quarrel with *him*. He's a gentleman, he is.'

Mrs Furze was impatient. She wanted to come to the point, and could not wait to manœuvre.

'I am afraid you and Tom do not get on together.'

'Well, Mrs Furze, if we don't it ain't my fault.'

'No, I dare say not; in fact, I am sure it is not. I dare say Tom is a little overbearing. Considering his origin, and the position he now occupies, it is natural he should be.'

'He ain't one as ought to give himself airs, marm. Why –'

Jim all at once dropped his chisel and his mask of indifference and flashed into ferocity.

'Why, my father was a tradesman, he was, and I was in your husband's foundry earning a pound a week when Master Tom was in rags. Who taught him, I should like to know?'

'Jim, you must not talk like that; although, to tell you the truth, Tom is no favourite of mine. Mr Furze, however, relies on him.'

'Relies on him, does he? Leastways, I know he does; just as if scores of others couldn't do jist as well, only they 'aven't 'ad his chance! Relies on him, as yer call it! But there, if I wur to speak, wot 'ud be the use?'

It is always a consolation to incapable people that their lack of success is due to the absence of chances. From the time of Korah, Dathan, and Abiram – who accused Moses and Aaron of taking too much upon themselves, because every man in the congregation was as holy as his God-selected leaders – it has been a theory, one may even say a religion, with those who have been passed over, that their sole reason for their supersession is an election as arbitrary as that by the Antinomian deity, who, out of pure wilfulness, gives opportunities to some and denies them to others.

'What do you mean, Jim? What is it that you see?'

'You'll excuse me, missus, if I says no more. I ain't a-goin' to meddle with wot don't concern me, and get myself into trouble for nothing: wot for, I should like to know? Wot good would it do me?'

'But, Jim, if you are aware of anything wrong it is your duty to report it.'

'Maybe it is, maybe it isn't; but wot thanks should I get?'

'You would get my thanks and the thanks of Mr Furze, I am sure. Look here, Jim.' Mrs Furze rose and shut the kitchen door. Phœbe was upstairs, but she thought it necessary to take every precaution. 'I know you may be trusted, and therefore I do not mind speaking to you. Tom's conduct has not been very satisfactory of late. I need not go into particulars, but I shall really be glad if you will communicate to me anything you may observe which is amiss. You may depend upon it you shall not suffer.'

She put two half-crowns into Jim's hand. He turned and looked at her with one eye partly shut, and a curious expression on his face – half smile, half suspicion. He then looked at the money for a few seconds and put it deliberately in his pocket, but without any sign of gratitude.

'I'll bear wot you say in mind,' he replied.

At this instant the kitchen door opened, and Phœbe entered. Mrs Furze went on with the conversation immediately, but it took a different turn.

'How do you think the old boiler became cracked?'

He was taken aback; his muddled brain did not quite comprehend the situation, but at last he managed to stammer out that he did not know, and Mrs Furze retired.

Jim was very slow in arranging his thoughts, especially after a sudden surprise. A shock, or a quick intellectual movement on the part of anybody in contact with him, paralysed him, and he recovered and extended himself very gradually. Presently, however, his wits returned, and he concluded that the pretext of the shop and business mismanagement was but very partially the cause of Mrs Furze's advances. He knew that although Mr Furze was restive under Tom's superior capacity, there was no doubt whatever of his honesty and ability. Besides, if it was business, why did the mistress interfere? Why did she thrust herself upon him? – 'coming down 'ere a purpose,' thought Mr Orkid Jim. 'No no, it ain't business,' and, delighted with his discovery so far, and with the conscious exercise of mental power, he smote the bricks with more vigour than ever.

'Good-bye, Phœbe,' said Catharine, looking in at the door.

'Good-bye, Miss,' said Phœbe, running out; 'hope you'll enjoy yourself: I wish I were going with you.'

'Where is she a-goin'?' asked Jim, when Phœbe returned.

'Chapel Farm.'

'Oh, is she? Wot, goin' there agin! She's oftener there than here. Not much love lost 'twixt her and the missus, is there?'

Phœbe was uncommunicative, and went on with her work.

'I say, Phœbe, has Catchpole been up here lately?'

'Why do you want to know? What is it to you?'

'Now, my beauty, wot is it to me? Why, in course it's nothin' to me; but you know he's been here.'

'Well, then, he hasn't.'

Phœbe, going to bed, had seen Tom and Catharine outside the gate.

'Wy, now, I myself see'd 'im out the night afore last, and I'd swear he come this way afore he went home.'

'He did not come in; he only brought Miss Catharine back from church: she'd gone there alone.'

Jim dropped his chisel. The three events presented themselves together – Tom's escort of Catharine, the interview with Mrs Furze, and the departure to Chapel Farm. He was excited, and his excitement took the form of a sudden passion for Phœbe.

'You're ten times too 'ansom for that chap,' he cried, and, turning suddenly, he caught her with one arm round her waist. She strove to release herself with great energy, and in the struggle he caught his foot in his tool basket and fell on the floor, cutting his head severely with a brick. Phœbe was out of the kitchen in an instant.

'You damned cat!' growled he, 'I'll be even with you and your Master Tom! I know all about it now.'

CHAPTER XV

As Jim walked home to his dinner he became pensive. He was under a kind of pledge to his own hatred and to Mrs Furze to produce something against Tom, and he had nothing. Even he could see that to make up a charge would not be safe. It required more skill than he possessed. The opportunity, however, very soon came. Destiny delights in offering to the wicked chances of damning themselves. It was a few days before the end of the quarter. The builder – in whose service Jim's brother, Joe, was – sent Joe to pay a small account for ironmongery, which had been due for some weeks. When he entered the shop Tom was behind his desk, and Jim was taking some instructions about a job. Mr Furze was out. Joe produced his bill, threw it across to Tom, and pulled the money out of his pocket. It was also market day; the town was crowded, and just at that moment Mr Eaton drove by. Tom looked out of the window on his left hand and saw the horse shy at something in the cattle pens, pitching Mr Eaton out. Without saying a word he rushed round the counter and out into the street, the two men, who had not seen the accident, thinking he had gone to speak to Mr Eaton. He was absent some minutes.

'A nice sort of a chap, this,' said Jim; 'he's signed your bill, and he ain't got the money.'

'S'pose I must wait, then.'

'Look 'ere, Joe: don't you be a b——y fool! You take your account. If he writes his name afore he's paid, that's *his* look-out.'

Joe hesitated.

'Wot are you a-starin' at? You've got the receipt, ain't yer? Isn't that enough? You ain't a-robbin' of him, for you never giv him the money, and I tell yer agin as he's the one as ought to lose if he don't look sharp arter people. That's square enough, ain't it?'

Joe had a remarkably open mind to reasoning of this description and, without another word, he took up the bill and was off. Jim also thought it better to return to the foundry. Mr Eaton, happily, was not injured, for he fell on a truss of straw, but the excitement was great; and, when Tom returned, Joe's visit completely went out of his head, and did not occur to him again, for two or three customers were waiting for him, and, as already observed, it was market day.

Now, it was Mr Furze's practice always to make out his accounts himself. It was a pure waste of time, for he would have been much better employed in looking after his men, and any boy could have transcribed his ledger. But no, it was characteristic of the man that he preferred this occupation – that he took the utmost pains to write his best copybook hand, and to rule red-ink lines with mathematical accuracy. Two days after the quarter a bill went to the builder, beginning, 'To account delivered'. The builder was astonished, and instantly posted down to the shop, receipt in hand, signed, 'For J. Furze, T. C.' Mr Furze looked at his ledger again, called for the day-book, found no entry, and then sent for Tom. The history of that afternoon flashed across him in an instant.

'That's your signature, Mr Catchpole,' said Mr Furze.

'Yes, sir.'

'But here's no entry in the day-book, and, what's more, there weren't thirty shillings that night in the till.'

'I cannot account for it, unless I signed the receipt before I had the money. It was just when Mr Eaton's accident happened, and I ran out of the shop while Joe was waiting. When I came back he had gone.'

'Which is as much as to say,' said the builder, 'that Joe's a thief. You'd better be careful, young man.'

'Well, Mr Humphries,' said Mr Furze loftily, 'we will not detain you: there is clearly a mistake somewhere; we will credit you at once with the amount due for the previous quarter, and if you will give me your account I will correct it now.'

Mr Furze took it, and ruled through the first line, altering the total.

'This is very unpleasant, Mr Catchpole,' observed Mr Furze, after the builder had departed. 'Was there anybody in the shop besides yourself and Joe?'

'Jim was there.'

Mr Furze rang a bell, and Jim presently appeared.

'Jim, were you in the shop when your brother came to pay Mr Humphries' bill about a week ago?'

'I wor.'

'Did he pay it? did you see him hand over the money?'

'I did, and Mr Catchpole took it and put it in the till. I see'd it go in with my own eyes.'

'Well, what happened then?'

'He locked the till all in a hurry, put the key in his waistcoat pocket; let me see, it wor in his left-hand pocket – no, wot am I a-sayin'? – it wor in his right-hand pocket – I want to be particklar, Mr Furze – and then he run out of the shop. Joe, he took up his receipt, and he says, says he, "He might a given me the odd penny," and says I, "He ain't Mr Furze, he can't give away none of the guvnor's money." If it wor the guvnor himself he'd a done it, and with that we went out of the shop together.'

'That will do, Jim; you can go.'

'Mr Catchpole, this assumes a very – I may say – painful aspect.'

'I can only repeat, sir, that I have not had the money. It is inexplicable. I may have been robbed.'

'But there is no entry in the day-book.'

It did not occur to Tom at the moment to plead that if he was dishonest he would have contrived not to be so in such a singularly silly fashion: that he might have taken cash paid for goods bought, and that the possibility of discovery would have been much smaller. He was stunned.

'It is so painful,' continued Mr Furze, 'that I must have time to reflect. I will talk to you again about it to-morrow.'

The truth was that Mr Furze wished to consult his wife. When he went home his first news was what had happened, but he forgot to mention the corroboration by Jim.

'But,' said Mrs Furze, 'Joe may have been mistaken; perhaps, after all, he did not pay the money.'

'Ah! but Jim was in the shop at the time. I had Jim in, and he swears that he saw Joe give it to Tom, and that Tom put it in the till.'

Mrs Furze seemed a little uncomfortable, but she soon recovered.

'We ought to have proof beyond all doubt of Tom's dishonesty. I do not see that this is proof. At any rate, it would not satisfy Catharine. I should wait a month. It is of no use making two faces about this business; we must take one line or the other. I should tell him that, on reconsideration, you cannot bring yourself to suspect him; that you have perfect confidence in him, and that there must be some mistake somewhere, though you cannot at present see how. That will throw him off his guard.'

Mr Furze acknowledged the superiority of his wife's intellect and obeyed. Tom came to work on the following morning in a state of great excitement, and with an offer of restitution, but was appeased, and Orkid Jim, appearing in the shop, was astonished and dismayed to find Tom and his master on the same footing as before. He went up to the Terrace, the excuse being that he called to see how the new boiler was going on. Phœbe came to the door, but he wanted to see the mistress.

'What do you want her for? She knows nothing about the boiler. It is all right, I tell you.'

'Never you mind. It wor she as give me the directions, worn't it, when I was 'ere afore?'

Accordingly the mistress appeared, and Phœbe, remaining in the kitchen, was sent upstairs upon some unimportant business, much cogitating upon the unusual interest Mrs Furze took in the kitchen range, and the evident desire on her part that her instructions to Jim should be private.

'Well, Jim, the boiler is all right.'

'That's more nor some things are.'

'Why, what has happened?'

'I s'pose you know. Joe paid Humphries' bill, and Mr Catchpole swears he never had the money, but Joe's got his receipt.'

'You were in the shop and saw it paid?'

'Of course I was. I s'pose you heerd that too?'

'Yes. We do not think, however, that the case is clear, and we shall do nothing this time.'

'I don't know wot you'd 'ave, Mrs Furze. If this 'ere ain't worth the five shillin' yer gave me, nothin' is – that's all I've got to say.'

'But, Jim, you must see we cannot do anything unless the proof is complete. Now, if there should happen to be a second instance, that would be a different thing altogether.'

'It ain't very comfortable for *me*.'

'What do you mean? Mr Furze sent for you, and you told him what you saw with your own eyes.'

'Ah! you'd better mind wot you're sayin', Mrs Furze, and you needn't put it in that way. Jist you look 'ere: I ain't very particklar myself, I ain't, but it may come to takin' my oath, and, to tell yer the truth, five shillin' don't pay me.'

'But we are not going to prosecute.'

'No, not now, but you may, and I shall have to stick to it, and maybe have to be brought up. Besides, it was put straight to me by the guvnor and Mr Tom was there a-lookin' at me right in my face. As I say, five shillin' don't pay me.'

'Well, we shall not let the matter drop. We shall keep our eyes open: you may be sure of that, Jim. I daresay you have been worried over the business. Here's another five shillings for you.'

Again Jim refrained from thanking her, but slowly put on his cap and left the house.

CHAPTER XVI

Mr Furze tried several experiments during the next two or three weeks. It was his custom to look after his shop when Tom went to his meals, and on those rare occasions when he had to go out during Tom's absence, Orkid Jim acted as a substitute. Whenever Mr Furze found a sovereign in the till he quietly marked it with his knife or a file, but it was invariably handed over to him in the evening. On a certain Wednesday afternoon, Tom being at his dinner, Mr Furze was summoned to the Bell by a message from Mr Eaton, and Jim was ordered to come immediately. He usually went round to the front door. He preferred to walk down the lane from the foundry, and when the back rooms were living rooms, passage through them was of course forbidden. As the summons, however, was urgent, he came the shortest way, and, looking in through the window which let in some borrowed light from the back of the shop to the warehouse behind, he saw Mr Furze, penknife in hand, at the till. Wondering what he could be doing, Jim watched him for a moment. As soon as Mr Furze's back was turned he went to the till, took out a sovereign which was in it, closely examined it, discovered a distinct though faint cross at the back of his Majesty George the Third's head, pondered a moment, and then put the coin back again. He looked very abstruse, rubbed his chin, and finally smiled after his fashion. Tom's shop coat and waistcoat were hung up just inside the counting-house. Jim went to them and turned the waistcoat pockets inside out. To put the sovereign in an empty pocket would be dangerous. Tom would discover it as soon as he returned, and would probably inform Mr Furze at once. A similar test for the future would then be impossible. Jim thought of a better plan, and it was strange that so slow a brain was so quick to conceive it. Along one particular line, however, the brain, otherwise so dull, was even rapid in its movements. It was Mr Furze's practice to pay wages at half-past five on Saturday afternoon, and he paid them himself. He generally went to his tea at six on that day, Tom waiting till he returned. On the following Saturday at half-past six Jim came into the shop.

'I met Eaton's man a minute ago as I wur goin' 'ome. He wanted to see the guvnor particklar, he said.'

This was partly true, but the 'particklar' was not true.

I told him the guvnor warn't in, but you was there. He said he was goin' to the Bell, but he'd call again if he had time. You'd better go and see wot it is.'

Tom took off his black apron and his shop coat and waistcoat, put them up in the usual place, and went out, leaving Jim in charge. Jim instantly went to the till. There were several sovereigns in it, for it had been a busy day. He turned them over, and again recognised the indubitable cross. With a swift promptitude utterly beyond his ordinary self, he again went to Tom's waistcoat – Tom always put gold in his waistcoat pocket – took out a sovereign of the thirty shillings there, put it in his own pocket, and replaced it by the marked sovereign. Just before the shop closed, the cash was taken to Mr Furze. He tied it carefully in a bag, carried it home, turned it over, and the sovereign was absent. Meanwhile Orkid Jim had begun to reflect that the chain of evidence was not complete. He knew Tom's habits perfectly, and one of them was to buy his Sunday's dinner on Saturday night. He generally went to a small butcher near his own house. Jim followed him, having previously exchanged his own sovereign for twenty shillings in silver. As soon as Tom had left the butcher's shop Jim walked in. He was well known.

'Mr Butterfield, you 'aven't got a sovereign, 'ave you, as you could give me for twenty shillings in silver?'

'Well, that's a rum 'un, Mr Jim: generally it's t'other way: you want the silver for the gold. Besides, we don't take many sovereigns here – we ain't like people in the High Street.'

'Mr Butterfield, it's jist this: we've 'ad overwork at the guvnor's, and I'm a-goin to put a sovereign by safe come next Whitsuntide, when I'm a-goin' to enjoy myself. I don't get much enjoyment, Mr Butterfield, but I mean to 'ave it then.'

'All right, Mr Jim. I've only two sovereigns, and there they are. There's a bran-new one, and there's the other.'

'I don't like bran-new nothin's, Mr Butterfield. I ain't a Radical, I ain't. Wy, I've seed in my time an election last a week, and beer a-runnin' down the gutters. It was the only chance a poor man 'ad. Wot sort of chance 'as he got now? There's nothin' to be 'ad now unless yer sweat for it: that Radicalism, that is, and if I 'ad my way I'd upset the b——y Act, and all the lot of 'em. No, thank yer, Mr Butterfield, I'll 'ave the old sovereign; where did he come from now, I wonder.'

'Come from? Why, from your shop. Mr Catchpole has just paid it me. You needn't go a-turnin' of it over and a-smellin' at it, Mr Jim; it's as good as you are.'

'Good! I worn't a-thinkin' about that. I wor jist a-lookin' at the picter of his blessed Majesty King George the Third, and the way he wore his wig. Kewrus, ain't it? Now, somebody's been and scratched 'im jist on the neck. Do yer see that ere cross?'

'You seem awful suspicious, Mr Jim. Give it me back again. I don't want you to have it.'

'Lord! suspicious! 'Ere's your twenty shillin's, Mr Butterfield. I wish I'd a 'undred sovereigns as good as this.' And Mr Jim departed.

Mr Furze lost no time in communicating his discovery to his wife.

'Furze,' she said, 'you're a fool: where's the sovereign? You haven't got it, but how are you to prove now that he has got it? We are just where we were before. You ought to have taxed him with it at once, and have had him searched.'

Mr Furze was crestfallen, and made no reply. The next morning at church he was picturing to himself incessantly the dreadful moment when he would have to do something so totally unlike anything he had ever done before.

On the Sunday afternoon Jim appeared at the Terrace, and Phœbe, who was not very well, and was at home, announced that he wished to see Mr Furze.

'What can the man want? Tell him I will come down.'

'I think,' said Mrs Furze, 'Jim had better come up here.'

Mr Furze was surprised, but, as Phœbe was waiting, he said nothing, and Jim came up.

'Beg pardon for interruptin' yer on Sunday arternoon, but I've 'eerd as yer ain't satisfied with Mr Catchpole, and I thought I'd jist tell yer as soon as I could as yesterday arternoon, while I was mindin' the shop, and he was out, I 'ad to go to the till, and it jist so 'appened, as I was a-givin' change, I was a-lookin' at a George the Third sovereign there, and took particklar notice of it. There was a mark on it. That werry sovereign was changed by Mr Catchpole at Butterfield's that night, and 'ere it is. I 'ad to go in there, as I wanted a sovereign for a lot of silver, and he giv it to me.'

'Can Butterfield swear that Catchpole gave it him?' said Mrs Furze, quite calmly.

'Of course he can, marm; that's jist wot I asked him.'

'That will do, Jim; you can go,' said Mrs Furze.

Jim looked at her, loitered, played with his cap, and seemed unwilling to leave.

'I'm comin' up to-morrow mornin', marm, just to 'ave one more look at that biler.' He then walked out.

'I suppose I must prosecute now,' said Mr Furze.

'Prosecute! Nothing of the kind. What is your object? It is to get rid of him, and let Catharine see what he is. Suppose you prosecute and break down, where will you be, I should like to know? If you succeed, you won't be a bit better off than you are now. Discharge him. Everybody will know why, and will say how kind and forgiving you are, and Catharine cannot say we have been harsh to him.'

Mr Furze was uneasy. He had a vague feeling that everything was not quite right; but he said nothing, and mutely assented to his wife's proposals.

'Then I am to give him notice to-morrow?'

'You cannot keep him after what has happened. You must give him a week's wages and let him go.'

'Who is to take his place?'

'Why do you not try Jim? He is rough, it is true, but he knows the shop. He can write well enough for that work, and all you want is somebody to be there when you are out.'

Mr Furze shuddered. That was not all he wanted, but he had hardly allowed himself, as we have already seen, to confess his weakness.

'It might be as well, perhaps,' added Mrs Furze, 'to have Tom up tomorrow and talk to him here.'

'That will be much better.'

It was now tea-time, and immediately afterwards Mr and Mrs Furze went to church.

Soon after nine on the following morning and before Mr Furze had left, Jim appeared with another request 'to see the missus.'

'I'll go downstairs,' she said. 'He wants to see me about the boiler.'

There was nobody but Jim in the kitchen.

'Well, Jim?'

'Well, marm.'

'What have you got to say?'

'No, marm, it's wot 'ave you got to say?'

'It is very shocking about Mr Catchpole, is it not? But, then, we are not surprised, you know; we have partly suspected something for a long time, as I have told you.'

' 'Ave you really? Well, then, it's a good thing as he's found out.'

'I am very sorry. He has been with us so long, and we thought him such a faithful servant.'

'You're sorry, are you? Yes, of course you are. Wot are yer goin' to do with him?'

'We shall not prosecute.'

'No, marm, you take my advice, don't yer do that; it wouldn't do nobody no good.'

'We shall discharge him at once.'

'Yes, that's all right; but don't you prosecute 'im on no account, mind that. *Mis-sis* Furze,' said Jim, deliberately, turning his head, and with his eyes full upon her in a way she did not like, 'wot am I a-goin to get out of this?'

'Why, you will be repaid, I am sure, by Mr Furze for all the time and trouble you have taken.'

'Now, marm, I ain't a-goin' to say nothin' as needn't be said, but I know that Tom's been a-makin' up to Miss Catharine, and yer know that as soon as yer found that out yer came and spoke to me. Mind that, marm; it was yer as come and spoke to me; it wasn't me as spoke fust, was it?' Jim was unusually excited. 'And arter yer spoke to me, yer spoke to me agin – agin I say it – arter I told you as I seed Joe pay the money, and then I brought yer that ere sovereign.'

Mrs Furze sat down. In one short minute she lived a lifetime, and the decision was taken which determined her destiny. She resolved that she would *not* tread one single step in one particular direction, nor even look that way. She did not resolve to tell a lie, or, in fact, to do anything which was not strictly defensible and virtuous. She simply refused to reflect on the possibility of perjury on Jim's part. Refusing to reflect on it, she naturally had no proof of it; and, having no proof of it, she had no ground for believing that she was not perfectly innocent and upright – a very pretty process, much commoner than perhaps might be suspected. After the lapse of two or three hours there was in fact no test by which to distinguish the validity of this belief from that of her other beliefs, nor indeed, it may be said, from that of the beliefs in which many people live, and for the sake of which they die.

'It is true, Jim,' said Mrs Furze, after a pause, 'that we thought Tom had so far forgotten himself as to make proposals to Miss Catharine, but this was a mere coincidence. It is extremely fortunate that we have discovered just at this moment what he really is; most fortunate. I have not the least doubt that he is a very bad character; your evidence is most decisive, and, as we owe so much to you, we think of putting you in Tom's place.'

Jim had advanced with wariness, and occupied such a position that he could claim Mrs Furze as an accomplice, or save appearances, if it was more prudent to do so. The reward was brilliant, and he saw what course he ought to take.

'Thank yer, marm; it was very lucky; now I may speak freely I may say as I've 'ad my eyes on Mr Catchpole ever so long. I told yer as much afore, and this ain't the fust time as he's robbed yer, but I couldn't prove it, and it worn't no good my sayin' wot I worn't sure of.'

This, then, is the way in which Destiny rewards those who refuse to listen to the Divine Voice. Destiny supplies them with reasons for discrediting it. Mrs Furze was more than ever thankful to Jim; not so much because of these additional revelations, but because she was still further released from the obligation to turn her eyes. Had not Jim said it once, twice, and now thrice? Who could condemn her? She boldly faced herself, and asked herself what authority this other self possessed which, just for a moment, whispered something in her ear. What right had it thus to interrogate her? What right had it to hint at some horrid villainy? 'None, none,' it timidly answered, and was silent. The business of this other self is suggestion only, and, if it be resisted, it is either dumb or will reply just as it is bidden.

'You can tell Mr Catchpole his master wishes to see him here.'

'Thankee, marm; good mornin'.'

Tom came up to the Terrace much wondering, and was shown into the dining-room by Phœbe not a little suspicious. Mr Furze sat back in the easy-chair with his elbows on the arms and his hands held up and partly interlaced. It was an attitude he generally assumed when he was grave or wished to appear so. He had placed himself with his back to the light. Mrs Furze sat in the window. Mr Furze began with much hesitation.

'Sit down, Mr Catchpole. I am sorry to be obliged to impart to you a piece – a something – which is very distressing. For some time, I must say, I have not been quite satisfied with the – the affairs – business – at the shop, and the case of Humphries' account made me more anxious. I could not tell who the – delinquent – might be, and, under advice, under advice, I resorted to the usual means of detection, and the result is that a marked coin placed in the till on Saturday was changed by you on Saturday night.'

A tremendous blow steadies some men, at least for a time. Tom quietly replied –

'Well, Mr Furze, what then?'

'What then?' said Mrs Furze, with a little titter; 'the evidence seems complete.'

'A marked coin,' continued Mr Furze. 'I may say at once that

I do not propose to prosecute, although if I were to take proceedings and to produce the evidence of Jim and his brother with regard to Humphries, I should obtain a conviction. But I cannot bring myself to – to – the – forget your past services, and I wish to show no unchristian malice, even for such a crime as yours. You are discharged, and there are a week's wages.'

'I am not sure,' said Mrs Furze, 'that we are not doing wrong in the eye of the law, and that we might not ourselves be prosecuted for conniving at a felony.'

Tom was silent for a moment, but it never entered into his head to ask for corroboration or any details.

'I will ask you both' – he spoke with deliberation and emphasis – 'do you, both of you, believe I am a thief?'

'Really,' said Mrs Furze, 'what a question to put! Two men declare money was paid to you for which you never accounted, and a marked sovereign, to which you had no right, was in your possession last Saturday evening. You seem rather absurd, Mr Catchpole.'

'Mrs Furze, I repeat my question: do you believe I am a thief?'

'We are not going to prosecute you: let that be enough for you; I decline to say any more than it suits me to say: you have had the reasons for dismissal; ask yourself whether they are conclusive or not, and what the verdict of a jury would be.'

'Then I tell you, Mrs Furze, and I tell you, Mr Furze, before the all-knowing God, who is in this room at this moment, that I am utterly innocent, and that somebody has wickedly lied.'

'Mr Catchpole,' replied Mrs Furze, 'the introduction of the sacred name in such a conjunction is, I may say, rather shocking, and even blasphemous. Here is your money: you had better go.'

Tom left the money and walked out of the room.

'Good-bye, Phœbe.'

'Are you going to leave, Tom?'

'Discharged!'

'I knew there was some villainy going on,' said Phœbe, greatly excited, as she took Tom's hand and wrung it, 'but you aren't really going for good?'

'Yes;' and he was out in the street.

'H'm,' said Mr Furze, 'it's very disagreeable. I don't quite like it.'

'Don't quite like it? – why, what *would* you have done? would you have had Catharine marry him? I have no patience with you, Furze!'

Mr Furze subsided, but he did not move to go to his business, and Mrs Furze went down into the kitchen. Mr Eaton had called at the shop at that early hour wishing to see Mr Furze or Tom. He was to return shortly, and Mr Orkid Jim, not knowing exactly what to do with such a customer, and, moreover, being rather curious, had left a boy in charge and walked back to the Terrace.

'There's Jim again at the door,' said Mrs Furze to Phœbe; 'let him in.'

'Excuse me, ma'am, but never will I go to the door and let that man in again as long as I live.'

'Phœbe! do you know what you are saying? I direct you to let him in.'

'No, ma'am; you may direct, but I sha'n't. Nothing shall make me go to the door to the biggest liar and scoundrel in this town, and if you don't know it yourself, Mrs Furze, you ought.'

'You do not expect me to stand this, Phœbe? You will have a month's wages and go to-night.'

'This morning, ma'am, if you please.'

Before noon her box was packed, and she too had departed.

CHAPTER XVII

Tom began to understand, as soon as he left the Terrace, that a consciousness of his own innocence was not all that was necessary for his peace of mind. What would other people say? There was a damning chain of evidence, and what was he to do for a living with no character?

He did not return home nor to the shop. He took the road to Chapel Farm. He did not go to the house direct, but went round it, and walked about, and at last found himself on the bridge. It was there that he met Catharine after her jump into the water; it was there, although he knew nothing about it, that she parted from Mr Cardew. It was no thundery, summer day now, but cold and dark. The wind was north-east, persistent with unvarying force; the sky was covered with an almost uniform sheet of heavy grey clouds, with no form or beauty in them; there was nothing in the heavens or earth which seemed to have any relationship with man or to show any interest in him. Tom was not a philosopher, but some of his misery was due to a sense of carelessness and injustice somewhere in the government of the world. He was religious after his fashion, but the time had passed when a man could believe, as his forefathers believed, that the earth is a school of trial, and that after death is the judgment. What had he done to be visited thus? How was his integrity to be discovered? He had often thought that it was possible that a man should be convicted of some dreadful crime; that he should be execrated, not only by the whole countryside, but by his own wife and children; that his descendants for ages might curse him as the solitary ancestor who had brought disgrace into the family, and that he might be innocent. There might be hundreds of such; doubtless there have been. Perhaps, even worse, there have been men who have been misinterpreted, traduced, forsaken, because they have been compelled for a reason sacredly secret to take a certain course which seemed disreputable, and the word which would have explained everything they have loyally sworn, for the sake of a friend, never to speak, and it has remained unspoken for ever. As he stood leaning over the parapet he saw Catharine coming along the path. She did not attempt to avoid him, for she wondered what he could be doing. He told her the whole story. 'Miss Catharine, there is just one thing I want to know: do you believe I am guilty?'

'I know you are not.'

'Thank God for that.'

Both remained silent for a minute or two. At last Tom spoke.

'Oh, Miss Catharine, this makes it harder to bear. You are the one person, perhaps, in the world now who has any faith in me; there is, perhaps, no human being at this moment, excepting yourself, who, after having heard what you have heard, would at once put it all aside. What do you suppose I think of you now? If I loved you before, what must my love now be? Miss Catharine, I could tear out my heart for you, and if you can trust me so much, why can you not love me too? What is it that prevents your love? Why cannot I alter it? And yet, what am I saying? You may think me honest, but how can I expect you to take a discharged felon!'

Catharine knew what Tom did not know. She was perfectly sure that the accusation against him was the result of the supposed discovery of their love for one another. If she had denied it promptly nothing perhaps would have happened. It was all due to her, then. She gazed up the stream; the leaden clouds drove on; the leaden water lay rippled; the willows and the rushes, vexed with the bitter blast, bent themselves continually. She turned and took her ring off her finger.

'It can never be,' she slowly said; 'here is my ring; you may keep it, but while I am alive you must never wear it.'

Tom took it mechanically, bent his head over the parapet, and his anguish broke out in sobs and tears. Catharine took his hand in hers, leaned over him, and whispered:

'Tom, listen – I shall never be any man's wife.'

Before he could say another word she had gone, and he felt that he should never see her again.

143

What makes the peculiar pang of parting? The coach comes up; the friend mounts; there is the wave of a handkerchief. I follow him to the crest of the hill; he disappears, and I am left to walk down the dusty lane alone. Am I melancholy simply because I shall not see him for a month or a year? She whom I have loved for half a life lies dying. I kiss her and bid her good-bye. Is the bare loss the sole cause of my misery, my despair, breeding that mad longing that I myself might die? In all parting there is something infinite. We see in it a symbol of the order of the universe, and it is because that death-bed farewell stands for so much that we break down. 'If it pleases God,' says Swift to Pope, 'to restore me to my health, I shall readily make a third journey; if not, we must part *as all human creatures have parted.*' As all human creatures have parted! Swift did not say that by way of consolation.

Tom turned homewards. Catharine's last words were incessantly in his mind. What they meant he knew not and could not imagine, but in the midst of his trouble rose up something not worth calling joy, a little thread of water in the waste: it was a little relief that nobody was preferred before him, and that nobody would possess what to him was denied. He told his father, and found his faith unshakable. There was a letter for him in a handwriting he thought he knew, but he was not quite sure. It was as follows:–

'DEAR MR CATCHPOLE, – I hope you will excuse the liberty I have taken in writing to you. I have left my place at the Terrace. I cannot help sending these few lines to say that Orkid Jim has been causing mischief here, and if he's had anything to do with your going he's a liar. It was all because I wouldn't go to the door and let him in, and gave missus a bit of my mind about him that I had notice. I wasn't sorry, however, for my cough is bad, and I couldn't stand running up and down those Terrace stairs. It was different at the shop. I thought I should just like to let you know that whatever missus and master may say, *I'm* sure you have done nothing but what is quite straight.

'Yours truly,

PHŒBE CROWHURST.'

Tom was grateful to Phœbe, and he put her letter in his pocket: it remained there for some time: it then came out with one or two other papers, was accidentally burnt with them, and was never answered. Day after day poor Phœbe watched the postman, but nothing came. She wondered if she had made any mistake in the address, but she had not the courage to write again. 'He may be very much taken up,' thought she, 'but he might have sent me just a line;' and then she felt ashamed, and wished she had not written, and would have given the world to have her letter back again. She had been betrayed into a little tenderness which met with no response. She was only a house-maid, and yet when she said to herself that maybe she had been too forward, the blood came to her cheeks; beautifully, too beautifully white they were. Poor Phœbe!

Tom met Mr Cardew in Eastthorpe the evening after the interview with Catharine, and told him his story.

'I am ruined,' he said: 'I have no character.'

'Wait a minute; come with me into the Bell where my horse is.'

They went into the coffee-room, and Mr Cardew took a sheet of note-paper and wrote:–

'MY DEAR ROBERT, – The bearer of this note, Mr Thomas Catchpole, is well known to me as a perfectly honest man, and he thoroughly understands his business. He is coming to London, and I hope you will consider it your duty to obtain remunerative employment for him. He has been wickedly accused of a crime of which he is as innocent as I am, and this is an additional reason why you should exert yourself on his behalf.

'Your affectionate cousin,

'THEOPHILUS CARDEW.

'To Robert Berdoe, Esq.,
        'Clapham Common.'

Mr Cardew married a Berdoe, it will be remembered, and this Robert Berdoe was a wealthy wholesale ironmonger, who carried on business in Southwark.

'You had better leave Eastthorpe, Mr Catchpole, and take your father with you. Are you in want of any money?'

'No, sir, thank you; I have saved a little. I cannot speak very well, Mr Cardew; you know I cannot: I cannot say to you what I ought.'

'I want no thanks, my dear friend. What I do is a simple duty. I am a minister of God's Word, and I know no obligation more pressing which He had laid upon me than that of bearing witness to the truth.'

Mr Cardew went off as usual away from what was before him.

'The duty of Christ's minister is, generally speaking, *to take the other side* – that is to say, to resist the verdicts passed by the world upon men and things. Preaching mere abstractions, too, is not by itself of much use. What we are bound to do is not only to preserve the eternal standard, but to measure actual human beings and human deeds by it. I sometimes think, too, it is of more importance to say *this is right* than to say *this is wrong*, to save that which is true than to assist into perdition that which is false. Especially ought we to defend character unjustly assailed. A character is something alive, a soul; to rescue it is the salvation of a soul!'

He stopped and seemed to wake up suddenly.

'Good-bye! God's blessing on you.' He shook Tom's hand, and was going out of the yard.

'There is just one thing more, sir: I do not want to leave Eastthorpe with such a character behind me – to leave in the dark, one may say, and not defend myself. It looks as if it were an admission I was wrong. I should, above everything, like to get to the bottom of it, and see who is the liar or what the mistake is.'

'Nobody would listen to you, and if you were to make a noise Mr Furze might prosecute, and with the evidence he has we do not know what the end might be; I will do my part, as I am bound to do, to set you right. But, above everything, Mr Catchpole, endeavour to put yourself where the condemnation of the world and even crucifixion by it are of no consequence.' Mr Cardew gave Tom one more shake of the hand, mounted his horse, and rode off. He had asked Tom for no proofs: he had merely heard the tale and had given his certificate.

Mr Furze distinctly enjoined Orkid Jim to hold his tongue. Neither Mr nor Mrs Furze wished to appear in court, and they were uncertain what Catharine might do if they went any further. Mr Orkid Jim had the best of reasons for silence, but Mr Humphries, the builder, of course repeated what he himself knew, and so it went about that Tom was wrong in his accounts, and all Eastthorpe affirmed him to be little better than a rascal. Mr Cardew, with every tittle of much stronger and apparently irresistible testimony before him, never for a moment considered it as a feather's weight in the balance.

'But the facts, my good sir, the facts; the facts – there they are: the receipt to the bill; Jim's declaration; his brother's declaration; the marked coin; the absolute proof that Catchpole gave it to Butterfield, and he could not, as some may think, have changed silver of his own for it, for Mr Furze paid him in gold, and there was not twenty shillings worth of silver in the till; what *have* you got to say? Do you tell me all this may be accident and coincidence? If you do, we may just as well give up reasoning and the whole of our criminal procedure.'

Mr Cardew did know the facts, *the* facts, and relying on them he delivered his judgment. Catharine, Phœbe, and Tom's father agreed with him – four jurors out of one thousand of full age; but the four were right and the nine hundred odd were wrong. In the four dwelt what aforetime would have been called Faith, nothing magical, nothing superstitious, but really the noblest form of reason, for it is the ability to rest upon the one reality which is of value, neglecting all delusive appearances which may apparently contradict it.

Tom left Eastthorpe the next morning, and on that day Catharine received the following letter from her mother:–

'MY DEAR CATHARINE, – I write to tell you that we have made an awful discovery. Catchpole has appropriated money belonging to your father, and the evidence against him is complete. (Mrs Furze then told the story.) You will now, my dear Catharine, be able, I hope, to do justice to your father and mother, and to understand their anxiety that you should form no connection with a man like this. It is true that on the morning when we spoke to you we did not know the extent of his guilt, but we had suspected him for some time. It is quite providential that the disclosure comes at the present moment, and I hope it will detach you from him for ever. Your father and I send our love, and please assure Mr and Mrs Bellamy of our regard.

'Your affectionate mother,

'AMELIA FURZE.'

On the same morning Mr Furze received the following note from Mr Cardew:–

'DEAR SIR, – I regret to hear that false charge has been preferred against my friend Mr Catchpole. By my advice he has left Eastthorpe without any attempt to defend himself, but I consider it my duty to tell you he is innocent; that you have lost a faithful servant, and, what is worse, you have done him harm, not only in body, but in soul, for there are not many men who can be wrongfully accused and remain calm and resigned. You ask me on what evidence I acquit him. I know the whole story, but I also know him, and I know that he cannot lie. I beg you to consider what you do in branding as foul that which God has made good. I offer no apology for thus addressing you, for I am a minister of God's Word, and I have to do all that He bids. I should consider I was but a poor servant of the Most High if I did not protest against wrong-doing face to face with the doer of it.

'Faithfully yours,

'THEOPHILUS CARDEW.'

Both Mr and Mrs Furze were greatly incensed, and Mr Cardew received the following reply, due rather to Mrs than to Mr Furze:–

'SIR, – I am greatly surprised at the receipt of your letter. You have taken up the cause of a servant against his master, and a dishonest servant, too: you have taken it up with only an imperfect acquaintance with the case, and knowing nothing of it except from his representation. If you were the clergyman of this parish I might, perhaps, recognise your right to address me, although I am inclined to believe that the clergy do far more harm than good by meddling with matters outside their own sphere. How can we listen with respect to a minister who is occupied with worldly affairs rather than with those matters which befit his calling and concern our salvation? Sir, I must decline any discussion with you as to Mr Catchpole's innocence or guilt, and respectfully deny your right to interfere.

'I am, sir,

'Your obedient servant,

'J. FURZE.'

Catharine's first impulse was to go home instantly and vindicate Tom, but she did not move, and the letter remained unanswered. What could she say to her own parents which would meet the case or would be worthy of such a conspiracy? She would not be believed, and no good would be done. A stronger reason for not speaking was a certain pride and a determination to retaliate by silence, but the strongest of all reasons was a kind of collapse after she arrived at Chapel Farm, and the disappearance of all desire to fight. Her old cheerfulness began to depart, and a cloud to creep over her like the shadow of an eclipse. Young as she was, strange thoughts possessed her. The interval between the present moment and death appeared annihilated; life was a mere span; a day would go by, and then a week, and in a few months, which could easily be counted, would come the end; nay, it was already out there, visible, approaching, and when she came to think what death really meant, the difference between right and wrong was worth nothing. Terrors vague and misty possessed her, all the worse because they were not substantial. She could not put into words what ailed her, and she wrestled with shapeless, clinging forms which she could hardly discern, and could not disentangle from her, much less overthrow. They wound themselves about her, and, although they were but shadows, they made her shriek, and at times she fainted under their grasp, and thought she could not survive. She had no peace. If soldiers lie dead upon a battle-field there is an end of them; new armies may be raised, but the enemy is at any rate weaker by those who are killed. It is not quite the same with our ghostly foes, for they rise into life after we think they are buried, and often with greater strength than ever. There is something awful in the obstinacy of the assaults upon us. Day after day, night after night, and perhaps year after year, the wretched citadel is environed, and the pressure of the attack is unremitting, while the force which resists has to be summoned by a direct effort of the will, and the moment that effort relaxes the force fails, and the besiegers swarm upon the fortifications. That which makes for our destruction, everything that is horrible, seems spontaneously active, and the opposition is an everlasting struggle.

At last the effect upon Catharine's health was so obvious that Mrs Bellamy was alarmed, and went over to Eastthorpe to see Mrs Furze. Mrs Furze in her own mind instantly concluded that Tom was the cause of her daughter's trouble, but she did not mean to admit it to her. In a sense Tom was the cause; not that she loved him, but because her refusal of him brought it vividly before her that her life would be spent without love, or, at least, without a love which could be acknowledged. It was a crisis, for the pattern of her existence was henceforth settled, and she was to live not only without that which is sweetest for woman, but with no definite object before her. The force in woman is so great that something with which it can grapple, on which it can expend itself, is a necessity, and Catharine felt that her strength would have to occupy itself in twisting straws. It is really this which is the root of many a poor girl's suffering. As the world is arranged at present, there is too much power for the mills which have to be turned by it.

Mrs Furze requested Mrs Bellamy to send back Catharine at once in order that a doctor might be consulted. She returned: she did not really much care where she was; and to the doctor she went. Dr Turnbull was the gentleman selected.

CHAPTER XVIII

Dr Turnbull was the doctor who, it will be remembered, lived in the square near the church. There was another doctor in Eastthorpe, Mr Butcher, of whom we have heard, but Dr Turnbull's reputation as a doctor was far higher than Mr Butcher's. What Eastthorpe thought of Dr Turnbull as a man is another matter. Mr Butcher was married, church-going, polite, smiling to everybody, and when he called he always said, 'Well, and how are *we*?' in such a nice way, identifying himself with his patient. But even Eastthorpe had not much faith in him, and in very serious cases always preferred Dr Turnbull. Eastthorpe had remarked that Mr Butcher's medicines had a curious similarity. He believed in two classes of diseases – sthenic and asthenic. For the former he prescribed bleeding and purgatives; for the latter he 'threw in' bark and iron, and ordered port wine. Eastthorpe thought him very fair for colds, measles, chicken-pox, and for rashes of all sorts, and so did all the country round. He generally attended everybody for such complaints, but as Mr Gosford said after his recovery from a dangerous attack, 'when it come to a stoppage, I thought I'd better have Turnbull,' and Mr Gosford sent for him promptly.

Dr Turnbull was born three or four years before the outbreak of the French Revolution. He was consequently a little older than the great Dr Elliotson, whose memory some of us still piously cherish, and Dr Elliotson and he were devoted friends. Dr Turnbull was tall, thin, upright, with undimmed grey eyes and dark hair, which had hardly yet begun to turn in colour, but was a little worn off his forehead. He had a curiously piercing look in his face, so that it was impossible if you told him an untruth not to feel that you were detected. He never joked or laughed in the sickroom or in his consulting-room, and his words were few. But what was most striking in him was his mute power of command, so that everybody in contact with him did his bidding without any effort on his part. He kept three servants – two women and a man. They were very good servants, but all three had been pronounced utterly intractable before they went to him. Master and mistress dared not speak to them; but with Dr Turnbull they were suppressed as completely as if he had been Napoleon and they had been privates. He was kind to them, it is true, but at times very severe, and they could neither reply to him nor leave him. He did not affect the dress nor the manners of the doctors who preceded him. He wore a simple, black necktie, a shirt with no frill, and a black frock-coat. The poor worshipped him, as well they might, for his generosity to them was unexampled, and he took as much pains with them and was as kind to them as if they were the first people in Eastthorpe. He was perhaps even gentler with the poor than with the rich. He was very apt to be contemptuous, and to snarl when called to a rich man suffering from some trifling disorder, who thought that his wealth justified a second opinion, but he watched the whole night through with the tenderness of a woman by the bedside of poor Phœbe Crowhurst when she had congestion of the lungs before she lived with Mrs Furze. He saved that girl and would not take a sixpence, and when the mother, overcome with gratitude, actually fell on her knees before him and clung to him and sobbed and could not speak, he lifted her up with a 'Nonsense, my good woman!' and quickly departed. He was a materialist, and described himself as one: he disbelieved in what he called the soap-bubble theory, that somewhere in us there is something like a bubble, which controls everything, and is everything, and escapes invisible and gaseous to some other place after death. Consequently he never went to church. He was not openly combative, but Eastthorpe knew his heresies, and was taught to shudder at them. His professionally religious neighbours of course put him in hell in the future, but the common people did not go so far as that, although they could not believe him saved. They somehow confounded his denial of immortality with his own mortality, and imagined he would be at an end when he was put into the grave. As time wore on the attitude, even of the clergy, towards the doctor was gradually changed. They hastened to recognise him on week-days as he walked in his rapid, stately manner through the streets, although if they saw him on Sundays they considered it more becoming to avoid him. He was, as we have seen, a materialist, but yet he was the most spiritual person in the whole district. He took the keenest interest in science; he was generous, and a believer in a spiritualism infinitely beyond that of most of his neighbours, for they had not a single spiritual interest. He was spiritual in his treatment of disease. He was before his age by half a century, and instead of 'throwing in' drugs after the fashion of Butcher, he prescribed fresh air, rest, and change, and, above everything, administered his own powerful individuality. He did not follow his friend Elliotson into mesmerism, but he had a mesmerism of his own, subduing all terror and sanative like light. Mr Gosford was not capable of great expression, but he was always as expressive as he could be when he told the story of that dreadful illness.

'He come into the room and ordered all the physic away, and then he sat down beside me, and it was just afore hay-harvest, and I was in mortal fright, and I said to him, "Oh, doctor, I shall die." Never shall I forget what I had gone through that night, for I'd done nothing but see the grave afore me, and I was lying in it a-rotting. Well, he took my hand, and he said, "Why, for that matter, my friend, I must die too; but there's nothing in it; you won't complain when you find out what death is. You won't die yet, though, and you'll get this lot of hay in at any rate; what a heavy crop it is!" and he opened the winder and looked out. The way he spoke was wonderful, and what it was which come into me when he said, '*I must die too,*' I don't know, but all my terrors went away, and I lay as calm as a child. 'Fore God I did, as calm as a child, and I felt the wind upon me across the meadow while he stood looking at it, and I could almost have got up that minute. I warn't out of bed for a fortnight, but I did go out into the hayfield, as he said.'

Why did Dr Turnbull come to Eastthorpe? Nobody ever knew while he lived. The question had been put at least some thousands of times, and all kinds of inquiries made, but with no result. The real reason, discovered afterwards, was simply that

153

he had bad health, and that he had fled from temptation in the shape of a woman whom he loved, but whom duty, as he interpreted it, forbade him to marry, because he considered it wicked to run the risk of bringing diseased children into the world.

This was the man to whom Catharine went. Mrs Furze went with her. He was perfectly acquainted with Mrs Furze, and had seen Catharine, but had never spoken to her. Mrs Furze told her story, which was that Catharine had no appetite, and was wasting, from no assignable cause. The doctor sounded her carefully, and then sat down without speaking. There was undoubtedly a weakness in one lung, but he was not satisfied. He knew how difficult it is to get people to tell the real truth to a physician, and that, if a third person is present, it is impossible. He therefore asked Mrs Furze if she would step into the next room. 'A girl,' he said, 'will not say all she has to say even to her mother'. Mrs Furze did not quite like it, but obeyed.

'Miss Furze,' said the doctor, 'I imagine you are a person who would not like to be deceived: you have a slight tenderness in the chest; there is no reasonable cause for alarm, but you will have to be careful.'

Catharine's face lighted up a little when the last sentence was half finished, and the careful observer noticed it instantly.

'That, however, is not the cause of your troubles: there is something on your mind. I never make any inquiries in such cases, because I know if I did I should be met with evasions.'

Catharine's eyes were on the floor. After a long pause she said –

'I am wretched: I have no pleasure in life; that is all I can say.'

'If there is no definite cause for it – mind, I say that – I may do something to relieve your distress. When people have no pleasure in living, and there is no concrete reason for it, they are out of health, and argument is of no avail. If a man does not find that food and light and the air are pleasant, it is of no use to debate with himself. Have you any friends at a distance?'

'None.'

'What occupation have you?'

'None.'

'It is not often that people are so miserable that they are unable to make others less miserable. If instead of thinking about yourself you were to think a little about those who are worse, if you would just consider that you have duties and attempt to do them, the effort might be a mere dead lift at first, but it would do you good, and you would find a little comfort in knowing at the end of the day that, although it had brought no delight to you, it had through you been made more tolerable to somebody. Disorders of the type with which you are afflicted are terribly selfish. Mind, I repeat it, I presuppose nothing but general depression. If it is more than that I can be of no use.'

Catharine was dumb, and Dr Turnbull's singular power of winning confidence was of no avail to extract anything more from her.

'I am sorry you cannot leave home. I shall give you no medicine. With regard to the chest, the single definite point, you know what precautions to take; as to the nervous trouble, do not discuss, ponder, or even directly attack, but turn the position, if I may so speak, by work and a determination to be of some use. If you were tempted by what you call wicked thoughts you would not nurse them. It is a great pity that people are so narrow in their notions of what wicked thoughts are. Every thought which maims you is wicked, horribly wicked, I call it. By the way, going to another subject, that poor girl Phœbe Crowhurst, who lived at your house, is very ill again. She would like to see you.'

Catharine left, and Mrs Furze came in.

'Has anything unsettled your daughter lately?'

'No, nothing particular.'

She thought of Tom, but to save Catharine's life she would not have acknowledged that it was possible for a Catchpole to have power to disturb a Furze. Had it been Mr Colston now, the case would have been different.

'She needs care, but there is nothing serious the matter with her. She ought to go away, but I understand she has no friends at a distance with whom she can stay. Give her a little wine.'

'Any medicine?'

'No, none; I should like to see her again soon; good morning.'

Phœbe's home was near Abchurch, and Catharine went over to Abchurch to see her, not without remonstrance on the part of Mrs Furze, Phœbe having been discharged in disgrace. Her father was an agricultural labourer, and lived in a little four-roomed, whitewashed cottage about a mile and a half out of the village. The living-room faced the north-east, the door opening direct on the little patch of garden, so that in winter, when the wind howled across the level fields, it was scarcely warmer indoors than outside, and rags and dish-clouts had to be laid on the door-sill to prevent the entrance of the snow and rain. At the back was a place, half outhouse, half kitchen, which had once had a brick floor, but the bricks had disappeared. Upstairs, over the living-room, was a bedroom, with no fireplace, and a very small casement window, where the mother and three children slept, the oldest a girl of about fourteen, the second a boy of twelve, and the third a girl of three or four, for the back bedroom over the outhouse had been given up to Phœbe since she was ill. The father slept below on the floor. Phœbe's room also had no fireplace, and great patches of plaster had been brought down by the rain on the south-west side. Just underneath the window was the pigstye. Outside nothing had been done to the house for years. It was not brick built, and here and there the laths and timber were bare, and the thatch had almost gone. Houses were very scarce on the farms in that part, and landlords would not build. The labourers consequently were driven into Abchurch, and had to walk, many of them, a couple of miles each way daily. Miss Diana Eaton, eldest daughter of the Honourable Mr Eaton, had made a little sketch in water-colour of the cottage. It hung in the great drawing-room, and was considered most picturesque.

'Lovely! What a dear old place!' said the guests.

'It makes one quite enamoured of the country,' exclaimed Lady Fanshawe, one of the most determined diners-out in Mayfair. 'I never look at a scene like that without wishing I could give up London altogether. I am sure I could be content. It would be so charming to get rid of conventionality and be perfectly natural. You really ought to send that drawing to the Academy, Miss Eaton.'

That we should take pleasure in pictures of filthy, ruined hovels, in which health and even virtue are impossible, is a strange sign of the times. It is more than strange; it is an omen and a prophecy that people will go into sham ecstasies over one of these pigstyes so long as it is in a gilt frame; that they will give a thousand guineas for its light and shade – light, forsooth! – or for its Prout-like quality, or for its quality of this, that, and the other, while inside the real stye, at the very moment when the auctioneer knocks down the drawing amidst applause, lies the mother dying from dirt fever; the mother of six children starving and sleeping there – starving, save for the parish allowance, for the snow is on the ground and the father is out of work.

Crowhurst's wages were ten shillings a week, and the boy earned half a crown, but in the winter there was nothing to do for weeks together. All this, however, was accepted as the established order of things. It never entered into the heads of the Crowhursts to revolt. They did not revolt against the moon because she was sometimes full and lit everybody comfortably, and at other times was new and compelled the use of rushlights. It was so ordained.

Half a mile beyond the cottage was a chapel. It stood at a cross-road, and no houses were near it. It had stood there for 150 years, gabled, red brick, and why it was put there nobody knew. Round it were tombstones, many totally disfigured, and most of them awry. The grass was always long and rank, full of dandelions, sorrel, and docks, excepting once a year in June when it was cut, and then it looked raw and yellow. Here and there was an unturfed, bare hillock, marking a new grave, and that was the only mark it would have, for people who could afford anything more did not attend the chapel now. The last 'respectable family' was a farmer's hard by, but he and his wife had died, and his sons and daughters went to church. The congregation, such as it was, consisted nominally of about a dozen labourers and their wives and children, but no more than half of them came at any one time. The windows had painted wooden shutters, which were closed during the week to protect the glass from stone-throwing, and the rusty iron gate was always locked, save on Sundays. The gate, the door, and the shutters were unfastened just before the preacher came, and the horrible chapel smell and chapel damp hung about the place during the whole service. When there was a funeral of any one belonging to the congregation the Abchurch minister had to conduct it, and it was necessarily on Sunday, to his great annoyance. Nobody could be buried on any other day, because work could not be intermitted; no labourer could stay at home when wife or child was dying; he would have lost his wages, and perhaps his occupation. He thought himself lucky if they died in the night.

The chapel was 'supplied,' as it was called, by an Abchurch deacon or Sunday-school teacher, who came over, prayed, preached, gave out hymns, and went away. That was nearly all that Cross Lanes knew of the 'parent cause.' The supplies were constantly being changed, and if it was very bad weather they stayed at home. On very rare occasions the Abchurch minister appeared on Sunday evenings in summer, but that was only when he wanted rest, and could deliver the Abchurch sermon of the morning, and could obtain a substitute at home.

Crowhursts had been buried at Cross Lanes ever since it existed, but the present Crowhursts knew nothing of their ancestors beyond the generation immediately preceding. What was there to remember, or if there was anything worth remembering, why should they remember it? Life was blank, blind, dull as the brown clay in the sodden fields in November; nevertheless, the Light which lighteth every man that cometh into the world shone into the Crowhurst cottage – that Light greater than all lights which can be lit by priest or philosopher, as the sun is greater than all our oil-lamps, gas, and candles. When Phœbe first had congestion of the lungs, not a single note of murmuring at the trouble caused escaped a soul in the household. The mother sat up with her at night, and a poor woman half a mile off came in during the day and saw that things went all straight. To be sure, there was Dr Turnbull. It was a long way out of his rounds, but he knew the Crowhursts well, and, as we have said, he watched over Phœbe as carefully as if she had been the daughter of a duke. Now Phœbe was ill again, but Dr Turnbull was again there, and although her cough was incessant, the care of father, mother, brother, and sister was perfect in its tenderness, and their self-forgetfulness was complete. It was not with them as with a man known to the writer of this history. His wife, whom he professed to love, was dying of consumption. 'I do not deny she suffers,' he said; 'but nobody thinks of *me*.' The sympathy of the agricultural poor with one another is hardly credible to fine people who live in towns. If we could have a record of the devotion of those women who lie forgotten under the turf round country churches throughout England, it would be better worth preserving than nine-tenths of our literature and histories. Surely in some sense they still *are*, and their love cannot have been altogether a thing of no moment to the Power that made them!

Catharine had never been to Phœbe's home before. At the Terrace she was smart, attractive, and as particular as her mistress about her clothes. Nobody ever saw Phœbe with untidy shoes or stockings, and even in the morning, before she was supposed to be dressed, her little feet were as neat as if she had nothing to do but to sit in a drawing-room. She was now lying on a stump bedstead with a patchwork coverlet over her, and to protect her from the draughts an old piece of carpet had been nailed on a kind of rough frame and placed between her and the door. Catharine's first emotion when she entered was astonishment and indignation. Therein she showed her ignorance and stupidity. The owner of the cottage did not force the Crowhursts to live in it. It was not he who directed that a girl dying of consumption should lie close to a damp wall in a room eight feet square with no ventilation. He had the cottage, the Crowhursts, presumably, were glad to get it, and he conferred a favour on them.

'Oh, Miss Catharine,' said Phœbe, 'this is kind of you! To think of your coming over from Eastthorpe to see me, and after what happened between me and Mrs Furze! Miss Catharine, I didn't mean to be rude, but that Orkid Jim is a liar, and it's my belief that he's at the bottom of the mischief with Tom. You haven't heard of Tom, I suppose, Miss?'

'Yes, he is in London. He is doing very well.'

'Oh, I am very thankful. I am afraid you will find the room very close, Miss. Don't stay if you are uncomfortable.'

Catharine replied by taking a chair and sitting by the bedside. There was somewhat in Phœbe's countenance, Catharine knew not what, but it went to her heart, and she bent down and kissed her upon the forehead. They had always been half-friends when Phœbe was at the Terrace. The poor girl's eyes filled with tears, and a smile came over her face like the sunshine following the shadow of a cloud sweeping over the hillside. Mrs Crowhurst came into the room.

'Why, mother, what are you doing here? You ought to be abed. Where is Mrs Dunsfold?'

'Mrs Dunsfold is laid up with the rheumatics, my dear. But don't you bother; we can manage very well. I will stay with you at night, and just a bit of sleep in the mornings. Your sister can manage after I've seen to father's breakfast and while I'm a-lying down, and if she wants me, she's only got to call.'

The mother looked worn and anxious, as though, even with Mrs Dunsfold's assistance, her rest had been insufficient.

'Mrs Crowhurst,' said Catharine, 'go to bed again directly. If you do not, you will be ill too. I will stay with Phœbe, at least for to-night, if anybody can be found to go to Eastthorpe to tell my mother I shall not be home.'

'Miss Catharine! to think of such a thing! I'm sure you sha'n't,' replied Mrs Crowhurst; but Catharine persisted, and a message was sent by Phœbe's brother, who, although so young, knew the way perfectly well, and could be trusted.

The evening and the darkness drew on, and everything gradually became silent. Excepting Phœbe's cough, not a sound could be heard save the distant bark of some farmyard dog. As the air outside was soft and warm, Catharine opened the window, after carefully protecting her patient. Phœbe was restless.

'Shall I read to you?'

'Oh, please, Miss; but there is nothing here for you to read but the Bible and a hymn-book.'

'Well, I will read the Bible. What would you like?'

Phœbe chose neither prophecy, psalm, nor epistle, but the

last three chapters of St Matthew. She, perhaps, hardly knew the reason why, but she could not have made a better choice. When we came near death, or near something which may be worse, all exhortation, theory, promise, advice, dogma fail. The one staff which, perhaps, may not break under us, is the victory achieved in the like situation by one who has preceded us; and the most desperate private experience cannot go beyond the garden of Gethsemane. The hero is a young man filled with dreams and an ideal of a heavenly kingdom which he was to establish on earth. He is disappointed by the time he is thirty. He has not a friend who understands him, save in so far as the love of two or three poor women is understanding. One of his disciples denies him, another betrays him, and in the presence of the hard Roman tribunal all his visions are nothing, and his life is a failure. He is to die a cruel death; but the bitterness of the cup must have been the thought that in a few days – or at least in a few months or years – everything would be as if he had never been. This is the pang of death, even to the meanest. 'He that goeth down to the grave,' says Job, 'shall return no more to his house, neither shall his place know him any more.' A higher philosophy would doubtless set no store on our poor personality, and would even rejoice in the thought of its obliteration or absorption, but we cannot always lift ourselves to that level, and the human sentiment remains. Catharine read through the story of the conflict, and when she came to the resurrection she felt, and Phœbe felt, after her fashion, as millions have felt before, that this was the truth of death. It may be a legend, but the belief in it has carried with it other beliefs which are vital.

The reading ceased, and Phœbe fell asleep for a little. She presently waked and called Catharine.

'Miss Catharine,' she whispered, drawing Catharine's hand between both her own thin hands, 'I have something to say to you. Do you know I loved Tom a little; but I don't think he loved me. His mind was elsewhere; I saw where it was, and I don't wonder. It makes no difference, and never has, in my thoughts, either of him or of you. It will be better for him in every way, and I am glad for his sake. But when I am gone – and I sha'n't feel ashamed at his knowing it – please give him my

Bible; and you may, if you like, put a piece of my hair in that last chapter you have been reading to-night.'

'Phœbe, my Phœbe, listen,' said Catharine: 'I shall never be Tom's wife.'

'Are you sure?'

'As sure as that I am here with my head on your pillow.'

'I am sorry.'

She then became silent, and so continued for two hours. Catharine thought she was asleep, but a little after dawn her mother came into the room. She knew better, and saw that the silence was not sleep, but the insensibility of death. In a few minutes she hurried Catharine downstairs, and when she was again admitted Phœbe lay dead, and her pale face, unutterably peaceful and serious, was bound up with a white neckerchief. The soul of the poor servant-girl had passed away – only a servant-girl – and yet there was something in that soul equal to the sun whose morning rays were pouring through the window. She lies at the back of the meeting-house, amongst her kindred, and a little mound was raised over her. Her father borrowed the key of the gate every now and then, and, after his work was over, cut the grass where his child lay, and prevented the weeds from encroaching; but when he died, not long after, his wife had to go into the workhouse, and in one season the sorrel and dandelions took possession, and Phœbe's grave became like all the others – a scarcely distinguishable undulation in the tall, rank herbage.

CHAPTER XIX

Catharine left the cottage that afternoon, and began to walk home to Eastthorpe. She thought, as she went along, of Phœbe's confession. She had loved Tom, but had reached the point of perfect acquiescence in any award of destiny, provided only he could be happy. She had faced sickness and death without a murmur; she had no theory of duty, no philosophy, no religion, as it is usually called, save a few dim traditional beliefs, and she was the daughter of common peasants; but she had attained just the one thing essential which religion and philosophy ought to help us to obtain, and, if they do not help us to obtain it, they are nothing. She lived not for herself, nor in herself, and it was not even justice to herself which she demanded. She had not become what she was because death was before her. Death and the prospect of death do not work any change. Catharine called to mind Phœbe's past life: it was all of a piece, and countless little incidents unnoticed at the time obtained a significance and were interpreted. She knew herself to be Phœbe's superior intellectually, and that much had been presented to her which was altogether over Phœbe's horizon. But in all her purposes, and in all her activity, she seemed to have had self for a centre, and she felt that she would gladly give up every single advantage she possessed if she could but depose that self and enthrone some other divinity in its place. Oh the bliss of waking up in the morning with the thoughts turned outwards instead of inwards! Her misery which so weighed upon her might perhaps depart if she could achieve that conquest. She remembered one of Mr Cardew's first sermons, when she was at Miss Ponsonby's, the sermon of which we have heard something, and she cried to herself, 'Who shall deliver me from the body of this death!'

Strange, but true, precisely at that moment the passion for Mr Cardew revived with more than its old intensity. Fresh from a deathbed, pondering over what she had learned or thought she had learned there – the very lesson which ought to have taught her to give up Mr Cardew – she loved him more than ever, and was less than ever able to banish his image from her. She turned out of her direct road and took that which led past his house – swept that way as irresistibly as a mastless hull is swept by the tide. She knew that Mr Cardew was in the habit of walking out in the afternoon, and she knew the path he usually took. She had not gone far before she met him. She explained what her errand had been, and added that she preferred the bypath because she was able to avoid the dusty Eastthorpe lane.

'I do not know those Crowhursts,' said Mr Cardew; 'they are Dissenters, I believe.'

The subject dropped, and Catharine had not another word to say about Phœbe.

'You look fatigued and as if you were not very well.'

'Nothing particular; a little cough at times, but the doctor says it is of no consequence, if I only take care.'

'You have been up all night, and you are now going to walk back to Eastthorpe?'

'Yes, the walk will refresh me.'

He did not ask her to go to his house. Catharine noticed the omission; hoped he would not – knew he would not.

'Have you heard anything of your father's assistant, Mr Catchpole?'

'Yes, he likes that situation which you obtained for him so kindly.'

'Is he quite happy?'

'Yes, I believe so.'

'I encountered Mr Colston, junior, a few minutes ago. He was on his way to Eastthorpe. I am afraid I was rather rude to him, for, to tell you the truth, I did not want his society. He is not an interesting young man. Do you care anything for him?'

'Nothing.'

'I should like to see the picture you have formed of the man for whom you would care. I do not remember' – speaking slowly and dreamily – 'ever to have seen a woman who would frame a loftier ideal.'

'He unconsciously came nearer to her; his arm moved into hers, and she did not resist.

'What is the use of painting pictures when reality is unattainable?'

'Unattainable! Yes, just what I imagined: you paint something unattainable to ordinary mortality. It is strange that most men and women, even those who more or less in all they do strive after perfection, seem to be satisfied with so little when it comes to love and marriage. The same sculptor, who unweariedly refines day after day to put in marble the image which haunts him, forms no such image of a woman whom he seeks unceasingly, or, if he does, he descends on one of the first twenty he meets and thinks he adores her. There is some strong thwarting power which prevents his search after the best, and it is as if Nature had said that we should not pick and choose. But the consequences are tremendous. I honour you for your aspirations.'

'You give me credit for a strength I do not possess, Mr Cardew. I said "unattainable". That was all. I did not say how.'

They had come to a gate which led out of the field into the road, and they paused there. They leaned against the gate, and Mr Cardew, although his arm was withdrawn from Catharine's, had placed it upon the top rail so that she felt it. The pressure would not have moved an ounce weight; there were half a dozen thicknesses of wool and linen between the arm and her shoulder, but the encircling touch sent a quiver through every nerve in her and shook her like electricity. She stood gazing on the ground, digging up the blades of grass with her foot.

'Do you mean,' said Mr Cardew, 'that you have ever seen him, and that – '

The pressure behind her was a little more obvious: he bent his head nearer to hers, looked in her face, and she leaned back on the arm heavily. Suddenly, without a word, she put both her hands to her head, pushed aside her hair, and stood upright as a spear.

'Good-bye,' she said, with her eyes straight on his. Another second and she had passed through the gate, and was walking fast along the road homewards alone. She heard behind her the

ɔound of wheels, and an open carriage overtook her. It was Dr
Turnbull's, and of course he stopped.

'Miss Furze, you are taking a long walk.'

She told him she had been to see Phœbe, and of her death.

'You must be very tired: you must come with me.'

She would have preferred solitude, but he insisted on her
accompanying him, and she consented.

'I believe I saw Mr Cardew in the meadow: I have just called
on his wife.'

'Is she ill?'

'Yes, not seriously, I hope. You know Mr Cardew?'

'Yes, a little. I have heard him preach, and have been to his
house when I was living at Abchurch.'

'A remarkable man in many ways, and yet not a man whom I
much admire. He thinks a good deal, and when I am in company
with him I am unaccountably stimulated, but his thinking is not
directed upon life. My notion is that our intellect is intended to
solve real difficulties which confront us, and that all intellectual
exercise upon what does not concern us is worse than foolish.
My brain finds quite enough to do in contriving how to remove
actual hard obstacles which lie in the way of other people's
happiness and my own.'

'His difficulties may be different from yours.'

'Certainly, but they are to a great extent artificial, and all the
time spent upon them is so much withdrawn from the others
which are real. He goes out into the fields reading endless books,
containing records of persons in various situations. He is not like
any one of those persons, and he never will be in any one of those
situations. The situation in which he found himself that morning at home, or that in which a poor neighbour found himself, is
that which to him is important. It is a pernicious consequence of
the sole study of extraordinary people that the customary
standards of human action are deposed, and other standards
peculiar to peculiar creatures under peculiar circumstances are
set up. I have known Cardew do very curious things at times. I
do not believe for one moment he thought he was doing wrong,
but nevertheless, if any other man had done them, I should have
had nothing more to say to him.'

'Perhaps he ought to have his own rules. He may not be constituted as we are.'

'My dear Miss Furze, as a physician, let me give you one word of solemn counsel. Nothing is more dangerous, physically and mentally, than to imagine we are not as other people. Strive to consider yourself, not as Catharine Furze, a young woman apart, but as a piece of common humanity and bound by its laws. It is infinitely healthier for you. Never, under any pretext whatever, allow yourself to do what is exceptional. If you have any originality, it will better come out in an improved performance of what everybody ought to do, than in the indulgence in singularity. For one person, who, being a person of genius, has been injured by what is called conventionality – I do not, of course, mean foolish conformity to what is absurd – thousands have been saved by it, and self-separation means mischief. It has been the beginning even of insanity in many cases which have come under my notice.' The doctor paused a little.

'I am glad Mrs Cardew is better,' said Catharine. 'I did not know she had been ill.'

'There is a woman for you – a really wonderful woman, unobtrusive, devoted to her husband, almost annihilating herself for him, and, what is very noteworthy, she denies herself in studies to which she is much attached, and for which she has a remarkable capacity, merely in order that she may the better sympathise with him. Then her care of the poor in his parish makes her almost a divinity to them. While he is luxuriating amongst the cowslips, in what he calls thinking, she is teaching the sick people patience and nursing them. She is a saint, and he does not know half her worth. It would do you a world of good now, Miss Furze, to live with her for six months if she were alone, but I am not quite sure that his influence on you would be wholesome. I was alarmed about her, but she will not die yet if I can help it. I want her to recover for her own sake, but also for her husband's and for her friends' sake. Perhaps I was a little too severe upon the husband, for I believe he does really love her very much; at least, if he does not, he ought.'

'Ought? Do you think, Dr Turnbull, a man ought to love what he cannot love?'

'Yes, but I must explain myself. I have no patience with people who seem to consider that they may yield themselves to something they know not what, and allow themselves to be swayed by it. A man marries a woman whom he loves. Is it possible that she, of all women in the world, is the one he would love best if he were to know all of them? Is it likely that he would have selected this one woman if he had seen, say, fifty more before he had married her? Certainly not; and when he sees other women afterwards, better than the one he has chosen, he naturally admires them. If he does not he is a fool, but he is bound to check himself. He puts them aside and is obliged to be satisfied with his wife. If it were permissible in him in such a case to abandon her, a pretty chaos we should be in. It is clearly his duty, and quite as clearly in his power, to be thus contented – at least, in nine cases out of ten. He *may* – and this is my point – he *may* wilfully turn away from what is admirable in his own house, or he may turn towards it. He is as responsible for turning away from it, or turning towards it, as he is for any of his actions. If he says he cannot love a wife who is virtuous and good, I call him not only stupid, but wicked – yes, wicked: people in Eastthorpe will tell you I do not know what that word means, because I do not go to church, and do not believe in what they do not believe themselves, but still I say wicked – wicked because he *can* love his wife, just as he can refrain from robbing his neighbour, and wicked because there is a bit of excellence stuck down before him for *him* to value. It is not intended for others, but for *him*, and he deserts the place appointed him by Nature if he neglects it.'

'You have wonderful self-control, Dr Turnbull. I can understand that a man might refrain from open expression of his love for a woman, whatever his passion for her might be, for, if he did not so restrain himself, he might mar the peace of some other person who was better than himself, and better deserved that his happiness should not be wrecked; but as for love, it may be beyond him to suppress it.'

'Well, Miss Furze,' replied the doctor, smiling, 'we are going beyond our own experience, I hope. However, what I have said is true. I suppose it is because it is my business to cure disease that I always strive to extend the realm of what is *subject* to us. You seem to be fond of an argument. Some day we will debate the point how far the proper appreciation even of a picture or a melody is within our own power. But I am a queer kind of doctor. I have never asked you how you are, and you are one of my patients.'

'Better.'

'That is good, but you must be careful, especially in the evening. It was not quite prudent to sit up last night at the Crowhursts', but yet, on the whole, it was right. No, you shall not get down here; I will drive you up to the Terrace.'

He drove her home, and she went upstairs to lie down.

'Commonplace rubbish!' she said to herself; 'what I used to hear at Miss Ponsonby's, but dressed up a little better, the moral prosing of an old man of sixty who never knew what it was to have his pulse stirred; utterly incapable of understanding Mr Cardew, one of whose ideas moves me more than volumes of Turnbull copy-book.'

Pulse stirred! The young are often unjust to the old in the matter of pulsation, and the world in general is unjust to those who prefer to be silent, or to whom silence is a duty. Dr Turnbull's pulse was unmistakably stirred on a certain morning thirty years ago, when he crept past a certain door in Bloomsbury Square very early. The blinds were still all drawn down, but he lingered and walked past the house two or three times. He had come there to take a last look at the bricks and mortar of that house before he went to Eastthorpe, under vow till death to permit no word of love to pass his lips, to be betrayed into no emotion warmer than that of man to man. His pulse was stirred, too, when he read the announcement of her marriage in the *Times* five years afterwards, and then in a twelvemonth the birth of her first child. How he watched for that birth! Ten days afterwards she died. He went to the funeral, and after the sorrowing husband and parents had departed he remained, and the most scalding tears shed by the grave were his. It was not exactly moral prosing, but rather inextinguishable fire just covered with a sprinkling of grey ash.

With that dreadful capacity which some people possess for

the realisation of that which is not present, the parting with Mr Cardew came before Catharine as she shut her eyes on her pillow: the arm was behind her – she actually felt it; his eyes were on hers; she was on fire, and once more, as she had done before, she cursed herself for what she almost called her cowardice in leaving him. She wrestled with her fancies, turned this way and that way: at times they sent the blood hot into her face, and she rose and plunged it into cold water. She was weary, but sleep was impossible. 'Commonplace rubbish!' she repeated: 'of what use is it to me?' She was young. When we grow old we find that what is commonplace is true. *We must learn to bear our troubles patiently*, says the copper-plate line for small text, and the revolving years bring nothing more. She heard outside a long-drawn breath, apparently just under the door. She opened it, and found Alice, her retriever. Alice came in, sat down by the chair, and put her head on her mistress's lap, looking up to her with large, brown, affectionate eyes which almost spoke. There is something very touching in the love of a dog. It is independent of all our misfortunes, mistakes, and sins. It may not be of much account, but it is constant, and it is a love for *me*, and does not desert me for anything accidental, not even if I am criminal. That is because a dog is a dog, it may be said; if it had a proper sense of sin it would instantly leave the house. Perhaps so, perhaps not: it may be that with a proper sense of sin it would still continue to love me. Anyhow, it loves me now, and I take its fidelity to be significant of something beyond sin. Alice had a way of putting her feet on her mistress's lap, as if she asked to be noticed. When no notice was taken she generally advanced her nose to Catharine's face – a very disagreeable habit, Mrs Furze thought, but Catharine never would check it. The poor beast was more than usually affectionate today, and just turned Catharine's gloom into tears. She was disturbed by a note from Dr Turnbull. He thought that what she needed was rest, and she was to go to bed and take his medicine. This she did, and she fell into a deep slumber from which she did not wake till morning.

Mr Cardew, when Catharine left him, walked homewards, but he went a long distance out of his way, much musing. As he went along something came to him – the same Something which had so often restrained Catharine. It smote him as the light from heaven smote Saul of Tarsus journeying to Damascus. His eyes were opened; he crept into an outhouse in the fields, and there alone in an agony he prayed. It was almost dark when he reached his own gate, and he went up to his wife's bedroom, where she lay ill. He sat down by the bed: some of her flowers were on a little table at her side.

'I am so ignorant of flowers, Doss (the name he called her before they were married); you really *must* teach me.'

'You know enough about them.'

He took her hand in his, put his head on the pillow beside her, and she heard a gasp which sounded a little hysterical.

'What is the matter, my dear? You are tired. You have walked a long way.'

She turned round, and then without another word he rose a little, leaned over her, and kissed her passionately. She never knew what his real history during the last year or two had been. He outlived her, and one of his sorrows when she was lying in the grave was that he had told her nothing. He was wrong to be silent. A man with any self-respect will not be anxious to confess his sins, save when reparation is due to others. If he be completely ashamed of them he will hold his tongue about them. But the perfect wife may know them. She will not love him the less: he will love her the more as the possessor of his secrets, and the consciousness of her knowledge of him and of them will strengthen and often, perhaps, save him.

CHAPTER XX

Mrs Cardew recovered, but Dr Turnbull recommended that as soon as she could be moved she should have an entire change, and at the end of the autumn she and her husband went abroad.

That winter was a bad winter for Mr Furze. The harvest had been the worst known for years: farmers had no money; his expenses had increased; many of his customers had left him, and Catharine's cough had become so much worse that, except on fine days, she was not allowed to go out of doors. For the first time in his life he was obliged to overdraw his account at the bank, and when his wife questioned him about his troubles he became angry and vicious. One afternoon he had a visit from one of the partners in the bank, who politely informed him that no further advances could be made. It was near Christmas, and it was Mr Furze's practice at Christmas to take stock. He set to work, and his balance-sheet showed that he was a poorer man by three hundred pounds than he was a twelvemonth before. Catharine did not see him on the night on which he made this discovery. He came home very late, and she had gone to bed. At breakfast he was unlike himself – strange, excited, and with a hunted, terrified look in the eyes which alarmed her. It was not so much the actual loss which upset him as the old incapacity of dealing with the unusual. Oh, for one hour with Tom! What should he do? Should he retrench? Should he leave the Terrace? Should he try and borrow money? A dizzy whirl of a dozen projects swung round and round in his brain, and he could resolve on nothing. He pictured most vividly and imagined most vividly the consequences of bankruptcy. His intellectual activity in that direction was amazing, and if one-tenth part of it could have been expended on the consideration of the next best thing to be done, not only would he have discovered what the next best thing was, but the dreadful energy of his imagination would have been enfeebled. He was sitting at his desk at the back of the shop with his head propped on his elbows, when he heard a soft footstep behind him. He turned round: it was Catharine.

'Dearest father,' she said, 'what is the matter? Why do you not tell me?'

'I am a ruined man. The bank refuses to make any further advances to me, and I cannot go on.'

Catharine was not greatly surprised.

'Look at that,' he said. 'I don't know what to do; it is as if my head were going wrong. If I had lost a lot of money through a bad debt it would be different, but it is not that: the business has been going down bit by bit. There is nothing before us but starvation.'

Catharine glanced at the abstract of the balance-sheet.

'You must call your creditors together and make a proposal to them. You will then start fair, and we will reduce our expenses. Nothing will be easier. We will live at the shop again; you will be able to look after things properly, and everything will go right – it will, indeed, father.'

She was very tender with him, and her love and counsel revived his spirits. Suddenly she was seized with a fit of coughing, and had to sit down. He thought he saw a red stain on the pockethandkerchief she put to her mouth.

'You shall not stay in this cold shop, my dear; you ought not to have come out.'

'Nonsense, father! There is nothing the matter. Have you a list of your creditors?'

'Yes; there it is.'

She glanced at it, and to her amazement saw Mr Cardew's name down for £100.

'Mr Cardew, father?'

'Yes; he came in one day, and said that he had some money lying idle, and did not know what to do with it. I was welcome to it if I wanted it for the business.'

A statement was duly prepared by Mr Askew, Mr Furze's solicitor; the usual notice was sent round, and the meeting took place in a room at the Bell. A composition of seven-and-sixpence in the pound was offered, to be paid within a twelvemonth, with a further half-crown in two years' time, the debtor undertaking to give up his house in the Terrace.

'Considering,' said the lawyer, 'that the debts owing to the estate are nearly all good, although just now it is difficult to realise, I think, gentlemen, you are safe, and I may add that this seems to me a very fair proposal. My client, I may say, would personally have preferred a different course, and would have liked to bind himself to pay in full at some future time, but I cannot advise any such promise, for I do not think he would be able to keep it.'

'I shall want some security for the half-crown,' said Mr Crook, representative of the firm of Jenkins, Crook and Hardman, iron merchants in Staffordshire.

'Can't say as I'm satisfied,' said Mr Nagle, brass founder. 'The debtor takes an expensive house without any warranty, and he cannot expect much consideration. I must have ten shillings now. Times are bad for us as well as for him.'

Mr Furze turned very white and rose to speak, but Mr Askew pulled him down.

'I beg, gentlemen, you will not take extreme measures. Ten shillings now would mean a sale of furniture, and perhaps ruin. My client has been a good customer to you.'

'I am inclined to agree with Mr Nagle,' said Mr Crook. 'Sentiment is all very well, but I do not see why we should make the debtor a present of half a crown for a couple of years. For my own part, if I want to be generous with my money, I have plenty of friends of my own to whom to give it.'

There was a pause, but it was clear that Mr Nagle's proposal would be carried.

'I am authorised,' said a tall gentleman at the back of the room, whom Mr Askew knew to be Mr Carruthers, of Cambridge, head of the firm of Carruthers, Doubleday, Carruthers and Pearse, one of the most respectable legal firms in the county, 'to offer payment in full at once.'

'It is a pity,' said Mr Nagle, 'that this offer could not have been made before. We might have been saved the trouble of coming here.'

'Pardon me,' replied Mr Carruthers; 'my client has been

abroad for some time, and did not return till last night.'

The February in which the meeting of Mr Furze's creditors took place was unusually wet. There had been a deep snow in January, with the wind from the north-east. The London coaches had, many of them, been stopped both on the Norwich, Cambridge, and Great North roads. The wind had driven with terrible force across the flat country, piling up the snow in great drifts, and curling it in fantastic waves which hung suspended over the hedges and entirely obliterated them. Between Eaton Socon and Huntingdon one of the York coaches was fairly buried, and the passengers, after being near death's door with cold and hunger, made their way to a farmhouse which had great difficulty in supplying them with provisions. Coals rose in Abchurch and Eastthorpe to four pounds a ton, and just before the frost broke there were not ten tons in both places taken together. Suddenly the wind went round by the east to the south-west, and it began to rain heavily, not only in the Eastern Midlands, but far away in the counties to the west and south-west through which the river ran. The snow and ice melted very quickly, and then came a flood, the like of which had not been seen in those parts before. The outfall has been improved since that time, so that in all probability no such flood will happen again. The water, of course, went all over the low-lying meadows. For miles and miles on either bank it spread into vast lakes, and the only mark by which to distinguish the bed of the stream was the greater rush and the roar. Cottages were surrounded, and people were rescued by boats. Every sluice and mill-dam were opened, but the torrent poured past them, and at Cottington Mill it swept from millpool to tail right over the road which divided them, and washed away nearly the whole garden. When the rain ceased the worst had to come, for the upper waters did not reach Eastthorpe until three or four days later. Then there was indeed a sight to be seen! The southern end of Eastthorpe High Street was actually two feet under water, and a man in a boat – event to be recorded for ever in the Eastthorpe annals – went from the timber-yard on one side of the street through the timber-yard gates and into the coal-yard opposite. Parts of haystacks, trees, and dead bodies of sheep and oxen drove down on the yellow, raging waves, and were caught against the abutments of the bridge. At one time it was thought that it must give way, for the arches were choked; the water was inches higher on the west side than on the east, and men with long poles stood on the parapet to break up the obstructions.

At last the flood began to subside, and on the afternoon of the day of the creditors' meeting Mr Orkid Jim appeared at the boathouse at the bottom of Rectory Lane and asked to be taken across. The stream was still very strong, but the meadows were clear, and some repair was necessary to the ironwork of a sluice-gate just opposite, which Jim wished to inspect before the men were set to work.

'Don't know as it's safe, Mr Jim,' said the boatman. 'It's as much as ever I can get through. It goes uncommon strong against the willows there.'

'You'll get through all right. I'll give yer a hand. I don't care to go a mile round over the bridge.'

'Yes, that's all very well, Mr Jim, but I don't want my boat smashed.'

'Smashed! I am a lucky one, I am. No harm comes to any boat or trap as long as I'm in it.'

The boatman consented. Just as he was about to push off, another man came down and asked for a passage. It was Tom Catchpole. Jim stared, but said nothing to him. The boatman also knew Tom, but did not speak. Jim now had half a mind to alter his intention of crossing.

'I don't know as I'll go,' said he. 'It does look queer, and no mistake.'

'Well, don't keep me a-waitin', that's all.'

Jim took his seat and went to the stern. Tom sat in the bow, and the boatman took the sculls. He had to make for a point far above the island, so as to allow for the current, and he just succeeded in clearing it. He then began to drift down to the landing-place in the comparatively still water between the island and the mainland. Jim stood up with a boat-hook in his hand and laid hold of an overhanging willow in order to slacken their progress, but the hook stuck in the wood, and in an instant the boat was swept from under him and he was in the water. He went down like a stone, for he could not swim, but rose again just as he was passing. Tom leaned over the side, managed to catch him by the coat-collar and hold his head above water. Fortunately the boat had swung round somewhat, and in a few seconds struck the bank. It was made fast, and in an instant Jim was dragged ashore and was in safety.

'That's a narrow squeak for you, Mr Jim. If it hadn't been for Mr Catchpole you'd have been in another world by this time.'

Jim was perfectly sensible, but his eyes were fixed on Tom with a strange, steady stare.

'Hadn't you better be moving and take off them things?'

Still he did not stir; but at last, without a word, he turned round and slowly walked away.

'That's a rum customer,' observed the boatman; 'he might have thanked us at least, and he hasn't paid me. Howsomever, I sha'n't forget it the next time I see him.'

Tom made no reply: gave the man double his usual fare, and went across the meadow. He had no particular object in coming to Eastthorpe, excepting that he had heard there was to be a meeting of Mr Furze's creditors, and he could not rest until he knew the result. He avoided the main street as much as possible, but he intended to obtain his information from Mr Nagle at the Bell.

As to Jim, he went home, changed his clothes and went out again. He walked up and down the street, and presently met Tom.

'Mr Catchpole,' he said, 'will you please come along o' me?'

There was something of authority in the tone of Jim's voice, and yet something which forbade all fear. Tom followed him in silence, and they went to the Terrace. Mr Furze was not at home, but Jim knew he would be back directly, and they waited in the kitchen, Tom much wondering, but restrained by some strange compulsion – he could not say what – not only to remain, but to refrain from asking any questions. Directly Mr Furze returned, Jim went upstairs, with Tom behind him, and to the amazement of Mr and Mrs Furze presented him in the dining-room.

'What is the meaning of this?' said Mrs Furze.

'Mrs Furze,' said Jim, 'will you please excuse me, and allow me to speak for this once? I don't see Miss Catharine here. I want yer to send for her. Wot I've got to say, I mean to say afore you all.'

Catharine was in her bedroom. She came down wrapped up in a shawl, and Jim stood up.

'Mr Furze, Mrs Furze, Miss Catharine, and you, Mr Catchpole, you see afore you the biggest liar as ever was, and one as deserves to go to hell, if ever any man did. Everything agin Mr Catchpole was all trumped up, for he never had Humphries' money, and it was me as put the marked sovereign in his pocket. I was tempted by the devil and by – but the Lord 'as 'ad mercy on me and 'as saved my body and soul this day. I can't speak no more, but 'ere I am if I'm to be locked up and transported as I deserve.'

'Never,' said Tom.

'You say never, Mr Catchpole. Very well, then: on my knees I axes your pardon, and you won't see me agin.' Jim actually knelt down. 'May the Lord forgive me, and do you forgive me, Mr Catchpole, for being such a – ' (Jim was about to use a familiar word, but checked himself, and contented himself with one which is blasphemous but also orthodox) – such a damned sinner.'

He rose, walked out, left Eastthorpe that night, and nothing more was heard of him for years. Then there came news from an Eastthorpe man, who had gone to America, that Jim was at work at Pittsburg; that he was also a preacher of God's Word, and that by God's grace he had brought hundreds to a knowledge of their Saviour.

This story may be deemed impossible by the ordinary cultivated reader, but he will please to recollect John Bunyan's account of the strange behaviour of Mr Tod. 'At a summer assizes holden at Hertford,' says Bunyan, 'while the judge was sitting up on the bench, comes this old Tod into court, clothed in a green suit, with his leathern girdle in his hand, his bosom open, and all in a dung sweat, as if he had run for his life; and being come in, he spake aloud as follows: "My Lord," said he, "here is the veriest rogue that breathes upon the face of the earth. I have been a thief from a child. When I was but a little one I gave myself to rob orchards, and to do other such like wicked things, and I have continued a thief ever since. My Lord, there has not been a robbery committed these many years, within so many miles of this place, but I have been either at it, or privy to it!" The judge thought the fellow was mad, but, after some conference with some of the justices, they agreed to indict him; and so they did of several felonious actions; to all of which he heartily confessed guilty, and so was hanged with his wife at the same time.' I can also assure my incredulous literary friends that years ago it was not uncommon for men and women suddenly to awake to the fact that they had been sinners, and to determine that henceforth they would keep God's commandments by the help of Jesus Christ and the Holy Spirit. What is more extraordinary is that they did keep God's commandments for the rest of their lives. Fear of hell fire and hope of heaven may have had something to do with their reformation, but these were not the sole motives, and even if they were, the strength of mind necessary in order to sacrifice the present for the sake of something remote – a capacity which lies, we are told, at the basis of all virtue – was singular.

CHAPTER XXI

Tom was restored to his former position, and Mr Furze's business began to improve. Arrangements were made for the removal from the Terrace, and they were eagerly pressed forward by Catharine. Her mother pleaded that they could not leave till June; that even in June they would sacrifice a quarter's rent, but Catharine's reply was that they would pay no more if they went beforehand. Her father was anxious to please her, and the necessary alterations at the shop were taken in hand at once, and towards the beginning of May were completed. She was not allowed to move to the High Street with her father and mother; it was thought that the worry and fatigue would be too much for her, and it was settled, as the weather was wonderfully warm and bright for the time of year, that she should go over to Chapel Farm for a week. At the end of the week she would find the furniture all in its place and her room quite straight. Mrs Bellamy called for her, and she reached the farm in safety, and looking better. The next morning she begged to be taken for a drive. Mr Bellamy had to go over to Thingleby, and she was able to go with him. It was a lovely sunny day, one of those days which we sometimes have in May, summer days in advance of the main body, and more beautiful, perhaps, than any that follow, because they are days of anticipation and hope, our delight in the full midsummer being sobered by the thought of approaching autumn and winter. When they reached the bridge Mr Bellamy remembered that he had forgotten his cheque-book and his money, and it was of no use to go to Thingleby without them.

'Botheration! I must go back, my dear.'

'Leave me here, Mr Bellamy; you won't be long. Let me get out, though, and just turn the mare aside off the road on to the grass against the gate; she will be quite quiet.'

'Had you not better sit still? I shall be back in a quarter of an hour.'

'If you do not mind, dear Mr Bellamy, I should so like to stand on the bridge. I cannot let the gig stay there.'

'Well, my dear, you shall have your own way. You know,' he said, laughing, 'I've long ago given up asking why my Catharine wants anything whatsomever. If she wishes it that's enough for me.'

Catharine dismounted, and Mr Bellamy walked back. She went to the parapet and once more looked up the stream. Once more, as on a memorable day in August, the sun was upon the water. Then the heat was intense, and the heavy cumulus clouds were charged with thunder and lightning. Now the sun shone with nothing more than warmth, and though the clouds, the same clouds, hung in the south-west, there was no fire in them, nothing but soft, warm showers. She looked and looked, and tears came into her eyes – tears of joy. Never had a day been to her what that day was. She felt as if she lay open to all the life of spring which was pouring up through the earth, and it swept into her as if she were one of those bursting exultant chestnut buds, the sight of which she loved so in April and May. Always for years when the season came round had she gathered one of those buds and carried it home, and it was more to her than any summer flower. The bliss of life passed over into contentment with death, and her delight was so great that she could happily have lain down amid the hum of the insects to die on the grass.

When they came back to the farm Mr Bellamy observed to his wife that he had not seen Catharine looking better or in better spirits for months. Mrs Bellamy said nothing, but on the following morning Catharine was certainly not so well. It was intended that she should go home that day, but it was wet, and a message was sent to Eastthorpe to explain why she did not come. The next day she was worse, and Mrs Bellamy went to East-thorpe and counselled Mr and Mrs Furze to come to the Farm, and bring Dr Turnbull with them. They all three came at once, and found Catharine in bed. She was feverish, and during the night had been slightly delirious. The doctor examined her carefully, and after the examination was over she turned to him and said –

'I want to hear the truth; I can bear it. Am I to die?'

'I know you can bear it. No man could be certain; but I believe the end is near.'

'How much time have I?'

He sat down by the bedside. 'Perhaps a day, perhaps a week. Is there anybody you wish to see?'

'I should like to see Mr Cardew.'

'Mr Cardew!' said Dr Turnbull to himself; 'I fancied she would not care to have a clergyman with her; I thought she was a little beyond that kind of thing, but when people are about to die even the strongest are a little weak.'

'She always liked Mr Cardew's preaching,' said Mrs Furze, sobbing, 'but I wish she had asked for her own rector. It isn't as if Mr Cardew were her personal friend.'

It was Saturday evening when the message was dispatched to Abchurch, but Mr Cardew was fortunately able to secure a substitute for the morrow. Sunday morning came. Mrs Furze, who had been sitting up all night, drew down the blinds at dawn, but Catharine asked, not only that they might be drawn up again, but that her bed might be shifted a little so that she might look out across the meadow and towards the bridge. 'The view that way is so lovely,' said she. It was again a triumphal spring day, and light and warmth streamed into the sick chamber.

Presently her mother went to take a little rest, and Mr Cardew was announced almost immediately afterwards. He came upstairs, and Mrs Bellamy, who had taken Mrs Furze's place, left the room. She did not think it proper to intrude when the clergyman visited anybody who was dying. Mr Cardew remained standing and speechless.

'Sit down, Mr Cardew. I felt that I should like to see you once more.'

He sat down by the bedside.

'Do you mind opening the window and drawing up the blind again? It has fallen a little. That is better: now I can see the meadows and away towards the bridge foot. Will you give me a glass of water?'

She drank the water: he looked steadily at her, and he knew too well what was on her face. Her hand dropped on the bed: he fell on his knees beside her with that hand in his, but still he was dumb, and not a single article of his creed which he had preached for so many years presented itself to him: forgiveness, the atonement, heaven – it had all vanished.

'Mr Cardew, I want to say something.'

'Wait a moment, let me tell you – *you have saved me*.'

She smiled, her lips moved, and she whispered –

'*You* have saved *me*.'

By their love for each other they were both saved. The disguises are manifold which the Immortal Son assumes in the work of our redemption.

Tom henceforth wore the ring on his finger. Mr Cardew resigned his living, and did not preach for many years. When pressed for an explanation he generally gave his health as an excuse. Later in life he took up his work again in a far distant, purely agricultural parish, but his sermons were of the simplest kind – exhortations to pity, consideration, gentleness, and counsels as to the common duties of life. He spent much of his time in visiting his parishioners and in helping them in their difficulties. Mrs Cardew, as we have said, died before him, but no woman ever had a husband more tender and devoted than hers in these later years. He had changed much, and she knew it, but she did not know exactly how, nor did she know the reason. It was not the kind of change which comes from a new theory or a new principle: it was something deeper. Some men are determined by principles, and others are drawn and directed by a vision or a face. Before Mr Cardew was set for evermore the face which he saw white and saintly at Chapel Farm that May Sunday morning when death had entered, and it controlled and moulded him with an all-pervading power more subtle and penetrating than that which could have been exercised by theology or ethics.

AFTERWORD

Catharine Furze is an English anti-Bovary. It presents a young woman who, like Emma Bovary, has grown up in the provinces surrounded by vulgar and simple people, at best honest farmers and servants, at worst schemers and snobs. Catharine has no education to speak of and, unlike Emma Bovary, she has no romantic notions. She has read very little – Milton, but not Shakespeare even – and she faces the emotional drama into which she is drawn with no resource but her own sense of what is right. To this she clings, without formulating or even explaining to herself what she is doing. For it is not a learnt system of morality, but something apparently quite instinctive – in this she is a characteristic Hale White heroine – and it saves her from committing any gross fault.

The book that bears her name is the quietest of Hale White's novels. It was written when he was sixty, in the immediate aftermath of the death of his wife, who had been a pitiful invalid for years, suffering from a progressive paralysis. As so often happens, death impelled the survivor to think back to the past, and the setting of *Catharine Furze* is the scene of Hale White's childhood, Bedford, here called Eastthorpe, in the 1840s. Very little in the book suggests an elderly author, and there is a special freshness about the descriptive writing; more than in any other of his books, the appeal of his native town and its surrounding landscape is stressed, with the ancient lanes, churches and shops, the broad, bright river, the outlying farms and hamlets in a level East Anglian countryside spread under open skies.

The story begins as though it were going to be a simple moralising provincial comedy in which a wise daughter rebukes the folly and pride of her foolish parents. Catharine is a cuckoo in the nest; she sees and feels what her parents do not, and she is quicker than they are, and has better instincts. Mr Furze is not a bad man, but he is severely limited; he has never taken a holiday from Eastthorpe, and he has never read a book in his life. He owns, through family inheritance, the largest ironmonger's shop and foundry in Eastthorpe, selling ploughs and agricultural instruments to all the farmers of the county, and his trade depends on his friendly links with the community. When we first see him he is drinking with his fellow shopkeepers and farmers on a Saturday afternoon, after giving them a 'market dinner'; this is a way of life that suits him and them; it is slow, and settled, like his allegiance to the nonconformist church of his forefathers.

Catharine is fond of her father, but has no great respect for him; for her mother she feels little affection even. Mrs Furze nourishes social ambitions of a petty but determined sort; the daughter of a Cambridge draper, she has been made ambitious by her girlhood proximity to the university, and is prepared to despise the trade that is her husband's livelihood. Hale White who, as a dissenter, had attended neither Oxford nor Cambridge, could not resist a joke at their expense when the chance arose, and Mrs Furze (a type of woman he knew and detested from his boyhood) is said to have a 'university flavour' clinging to her, although she is quite uneducated. But whereas Furze is merely a fool, Mrs Furze has method in her folly and schemes to disastrous effect to get her own way. Sometimes her efforts are unavailing, and purely comic, as when she tries to throw Catharine into the company of a supposedly eligible but detestable young man; sometimes they are more effective and therefore dangerous, as when she persuades her husband to desert chapel for socially superior church, and to move from the shop above which his family has always lived into a genteel house on the outskirts of town – a place characterised by her daughter as a 'filthy, stuck-up, stuccoed hovel'.

Mrs Furze's taste and instincts are equally false. She banishes the solid old furniture and the paintings of George IV, the Virgin Mary and the squire in his hunting clothes to the spare bedroom of her new house, and hangs instead vaguely 'Continental' oleographs of sunsets and full moons. Similarly, she has no glimmer of understanding of her daughter's friendship for the farming Bellamys, who give her the freedom of the natural world, or Tom the apprentice, who is young and clever, or Phoebe, her honest and honourable maid. These good people are the closest companions Catharine has, but they do not answer all her needs. There is nothing in Eastthorpe to relieve her sense of mental isolation. 'Often she knew what it was to thirst like one in a desert for human intercourse'; 'she stood by herself, affiliated to nothing, an individual belonging to no species'; 'when she was in ordinary Eastthorpe society she felt as a pent-up lake might feel if the weight of its waters were used in threading needles' – a vivid and passionate image highly characteristic of this pent-up book.

Catharine is by nature a lively and thoughtful young woman, but she has nothing whatsoever to occupy herself with except the prospect of marriage one day to a local youth; no culture, no intimate friends, no real education, no alternative direction in which to turn. (Hale White suggests that she would have found life better two hundred years earlier, in the days of religious enthusiasm, rather as George Eliot suggests in *Middlemarch* that Dorothea is a St Teresa without a vocation; Hale White also adds that Catharine would have done better in a later generation, when she would have had the 'opiate' of an education.) When she meets Mr Cardew, the young clergyman who finds his wife dull and is drawn to Catharine, she is vulnerable because he is the first man who has addressed her with a shared intellectual interest: 'St Paul and Milton in him saluted St Paul and Milton in her.' Milton, the Bible and the martyrdom of the Roman Christians (Cardew gives her a preposterously romantic story he has written on this theme) may seem strange wooing material, but it was the material at hand, and it was enough to transform her. Hale White describes the process as the natural phenomenon it is:

She began now to look forward to Sunday with intense expectation; a new motive for life was supplied to her, and a new force urged her through each day. It was with her as we can imagine it to to be with some bud long folded in darkness which, silently in the dewy May night, loosens its leaves, and, as the sun rises, bares itself to the depths of its cup to the blue sky and the light.

The relationship between Catharine and Cardew, although it amounts to nothing more than a few conversations, a pressure on the arm, a failure to meet on a summer night, is intense and erotic. It arouses 'the very life of all that was Catharine, senses, heart, and intellect, a summing-up and projection of her whole selfhood'. The sexual temptation is made quite explicit (Hale White links it at one moment to a thunderstorm, as he does in his later novel *Clara Hopgood*, in which the lovers succumb to temptation). Hale White makes the reader feel both that it is unimaginable – he talks of a common, criminal act – and deeply imagined and enjoyed by both Cardew and Catharine.

The account of Cardew is interestingly balanced between distaste and sympathy throughout the book. He is thirty-five, good-looking and short-sighted, ultra-Evangelical, a theological theorist who knows nothing of real humanity as yet. But this is not entirely his own fault; the only son of a doting and religious mother, he has been pushed into Cambridge and the church to satisfy her ambitions and pushed into an early marriage with the daughter of her best friend. Quite unable to defend himself against his mother's will, with no experience of women, says Hale White, 'he fell in love with himself, married himself, and soon after discovered that he did not know who his wife was'. The formulation is brilliantly applicable to many early marriages. Cardew, like Catharine, is suffering from isolation when they meet.

It is not the fault of young Mrs Cardew. She appears at first as dull and nervous; then as gentle and good; and presently we learn that she has yet another wasted intellect, for she has a scientific bent which is of course doomed to wither in a clergyman's wife in 1840: 'at that time there was no outlet for any womanly faculty, much larger in quantity than we are apt to suppose, which has an appetite for exact facts,' notes Hale White. Catharine herself is quick to see Jane Cardew's virtues, and her sisterly feelings work powerfully in her. But none of the three intelligent women in the book – Jane, Catharine and the Furzes' maid Phoebe – is able to find any satisfactory outlet for her mental energies. Each of them has, in Hale White's phrase, 'too much power for the mills which have to be turned' and each of them turns away from life, either resigned to or willing death at different points in the narrative. One may feel that Hale White, being subject to black depression himself, allowed this to seep into his book; or one may think that he was making a perfectly just observation about the effect of social conditions on clever young women – the Brontë family may be taken as a case in point. The kind of constraint that Florence Nightingale raged against in her document *Cassandra* was felt by thousands of others, less rich, less articulate, less original in seeking outlets and solutions, but no less sensitive to the waste of their spirits and abilities. Hale White proclaimed no overtly feminist purpose in his writing, but he was keenly aware of the cramping and numbing process endured by women.

His choice of entirely insignificant young women is in line with his particular sympathy with obscure suffering, with lives that go by and slip away unrecorded. He would have liked E. P. Thompson's remark about people who need to be rescued from the condescension of history. Early in his book Hale White muses on some ancient, unattributed skulls found near Eastthorpe; from them he turns to the bones in the churchyards, jostled anonymously together; and from there to mention that a bloody skirmish had taken place during the Civil War, but that no record of who was killed or who won survives. 'Nevertheless,' he goes on, 'Eastthorpe had really had a history. It had known victory and defeat, love, hatred, intrigue, hope, despair, and all the passions, just as Elizabeth, King Charles, Cromwell and Queen Anne knew them, but they were not recorded.' Another passage towards the end of the book takes up these sentiments again, this time with more pathos, when he describes a nonconformist graveyard in a hamlet outside Eastthorpe, where Phoebe's forebears lie; here the people are mostly too poor to put up memorial stones. The sorrel, docks and dandelions in the rank grass, the unnamed and fast-disappearing mounds are intensely sad, because they seem to efface far too quickly that individuality which is so precious to the puritan ethos.

One obviously incongruous feature in the book is the introduction of a piece of skullduggery of the kind Dickens might just have got away with, but Hale White simply cannot; he lacks the robust energy. The character of 'Orkid Jim', who is involved in this plotting, never grows into anything more than the stock envious and dishonest workman of a hundred cautionary tales, and his sudden conversion is no more convincing than his villainy. Still, it is slightly more interesting, because it bears the stamp of Hale White's Bedford and puritan past, by alluding to Bunyan, Bedford's greatest citizen. Hale White loved Bunyan's work – he wrote a biographical study of him – and invokes his name more than once in *Catharine Furze*. Orkid Jim is a far cry from the *Pilgrim's Progress* or *Mr Badman*, but the moral struggles, fear of retribution and sudden, dramatic changes of heart that appear so vividly in Bunyan do at least provide some sort of context for Jim's behaviour.

Another awkwardness is the introduction of the good Dr Turnbull, a stock Hale White voice of virtue: Turnbull is a freethinker, born before the French Revolution, good to the poor and short with the rich, 'spiritual in his treatment of disease' and with an early interest in eugenics. Beyond this, he serves no function but to say sound things and to be notably unsuccessful in caring for his young female patients.

But neither Orkid Jim nor Dr Turnbull can spoil the charm of *Catharine Furze*. It is the most poetic of Hale White's novels. Its pastoral and idyllic aspect, although menaced from the start, is touching and beautiful. The comedy of provincial pretensions is well observed. The aspect of adultery in an enclosed and rigidly patterned community is approached boldly and painfully; and there is a developed tragedy in the wastage of the brightest and the best.

It is the novel of Hale White's that makes one understand most clearly why D. H. Lawrence found so much to admire in his work. Here Lawrence found what he also had, a close knowledge of the life of the provincial poor, a passionate appreciation of the countryside – for both, farms have an almost religious value – and a horror of the stifling effect of gentility. Both writers present experience in terms of progress from one moment of intensity to another; and both show a tender and profound sympathy with women – so close that it might be better called empathy.

Claire Tomalin, London 1984

THE HOGARTH PRESS

A New Life For A Great Name

This is a paperback list for today's readers – but it holds to a tradition of adventurous and original publishing set by Leonard and Virginia Woolf when they founded The Hogarth Press in 1917 and started their first paperback series in 1924.

Now, after many years of partnership, Chatto & Windus · The Hogarth Press are proud to launch this new series. Our choice of books does not echo that of the Woolfs in every way – times have changed – but our aims are the same. Some sections of the list are light-hearted, some serious: all are rigorously chosen, excellently produced and energetically published, in the best Hogarth Press tradition. We hope that the new Hogarth Press paperback list will be as prized – and as avidly collected – as its illustrious forebear.

A list of our books already published, together with some of our forthcoming titles, follows. If you would like more information about Hogarth Press books, write to us for a catalogue:

40 William IV Street, London WC2N 4DF

Please send a large stamped addressed envelope

HOGARTH FICTION

Death of a Hero by Richard Aldington
New Introduction by Christopher Ridgway

Epitaph of a Small Winner by Machado de Assis
Translated and introduced by William L. Grossman

Chance by Joseph Conrad
New Introduction by Jane Miller

The Whirlpool by George Gissing
New Introduction by Gillian Tindall

Mr Weston's Good Wine by T. F. Powys
New Introduction by Ronald Blythe

Catharine Furze by Mark Rutherford
Clara Hopgood by Mark Rutherford
The Revolution in Tanner's Lane by Mark Rutherford
New Introductions by Claire Tomalin

Christina Alberta's Father by H. G. Wells
Mr Britling Sees It Through by H. G. Wells
New Introductions by Christopher Priest

Frank Burnet by Dorothy Vernon White
New Afterword by Irvin Stock

HOGARTH HUMOUR

The Amazing Test Match Crime by Adrian Alington
New Introduction by Brian Johnston

Mrs Ames by E. F. Benson
Paying Guests by E. F. Benson
Secret Lives by E. F. Benson
New Introductions by Stephen Pile

Vestal Fire by Compton Mackenzie
New Introduction by Sally Beauman

HOGARTH LITERARY CRITICISM

Seven Types of Ambiguity by William Empson

The Common Pursuit by F. R. Leavis

By Way of Sainte-Beuve by Marcel Proust
Translated by Sylvia Townsend Warner
New Introduction by Terence Kilmartin

The English Novel from Dickens to Lawrence by
Raymond Williams

The Common Reader, First Series by Virginia Woolf
Edited and introduced by Andrew McNeillie

HOGARTH POETRY

The Complete Poems 1927-1979, Elizabeth Bishop

Collected Poems, C. P. Cavafy
Translated by Edmund Keeley and Philip Sherrard
Edited by George Savidis

Collected Poems, William Empson

HOGARTH TRAVEL

Now I Remember: A Holiday History of England by
Ronald Hamilton

The Spanish Temper by V. S. Pritchett
New Introduction by the Author

The Amateur Emigrant by Robert Louis Stevenson
New Introduction by Jonathan Raban

HOGARTH CRIME

The Beckoning Lady by Margery Allingham

Hide My Eyes by Margery Allingham

Dead Mrs Stratton by Anthony Berkeley

The Baffle Book edited by F. Tennyson Jesse

Death by Request by Romilly and Katherine John

The Saltmarsh Murders by Gladys Mitchell

The Hand in The Glove by Rex Stout

HOGARTH BIOGRAPHY AND AUTOBIOGRAPHY

The Journal of a Disappointed Man & A Last Diary by
W. N. P. Barbellion
Original Introduction by H. G. Wells and New Introduction by
Deborah Singmaster

Samuel Johnson by Walter Jackson Bate

Still Life: Sketches from a Tunbridge Wells Childhood by
Richard Cobb

Ivor Gurney: War Letters
A selection edited by R. K. R. Thornton

Being Geniuses Together, 1920-1930 by Robert McAlmon and
Kay Boyle
New Afterword by Kay Boyle

The Smith of Smiths by Hesketh Pearson
New Introduction by Richard Ingrams

HOGARTH FICTION

Mark Rutherford

The Revolution in Tanner's Lane

New Introduction by Claire Tomalin

'I've read the *Revolution in Tanner's Lane*, and find myself fearfully fond of Rutherford' – *D.H. Lawrence*

This story of one man's fortitude in the face of private and public adversity is set in the early years of the Industrial Revolution. It presents a compelling portrait of its time yet, like the work of Dickens, is much more than an indispensable chapter of social history: a compassionate and absorbing novel, *The Revolution in Tanner's Lane* is a classic of nineteenth-century literature.

T.F. Powys
Mr Weston's Good Wine
New Introduction by Ronald Blythe

Mr Weston is no ordinary salesman, as various portents make clear when he arrives in Folly Down. For Mr Weston is nothing less than God made flesh, and the simple, inspiring tale of his visit to a quite normal village is a realistic allegory almost without parallel in modern literature. Ironic and comic, this masterpiece by the brother of John Cowper and Llewelyn Powys was first published in 1927.

Joseph Conrad

Chance

New Introduction by Jane Miller

'Being a woman is a terribly difficult trade since it consists principally of dealings with men . . .'

Narrated by Marlowe – encountered before in *Lord Jim* and *The Heart of Darkness* – *Chance* contains many of Conrad's most penetrating observations of women and their role in society. The story of a doomed love affair, it was the author's only attempt to address directly the subject of feminism and his first great commercial success.

George Gissing
The Whirlpool
New Introduction by Gillian Tindall

'Marriage rarely means happiness, either for man or woman . . .'

In *The Whirlpool* George Gissing explores sympathetically, but without illusions, his vision of married life: an existence often leading to 'envy, hatred, fear'. This magnificent novel, a masterpiece of English social realism, is a powerful diagnosis of human institutions and the suffering of those caught up in them.